Bike Share

There are now over 2,000 cities with a bike share program. *Bike Share* examines all the major developments in the 50-year history of bike share. The book provides a detailed focus on contemporary bike share programs, including many of the most prominent systems, such as those in Paris, London and New York, as well as the rapidly emerging dockless bike share sector. This book also addresses how rapid technological innovation, particularly in terms of mobile Internet devices and electric assist bicycles, may change the face of not just cycling, but urban mobility more generally.

By the end of 2018, it was estimated that there are more than 20 million bicycles in the global bike share fleet, with most of these dockless, coming online only in the last 3 years. Consequently, research examining bike share has not kept pace with the rapid deployment of this new form of urban mobility.

Bike Share addresses a number of key themes such as the following:

- The urban age, contextualising bike share within a wider urbanism movement and how it sits within the growing sharing economy.
- The impact of bike share, looking at systems in China, Europe, North America and Australia to see how these programs have changed travel patterns and consequent impact on car use, emissions, congestion, public health and safety.
- The bike share business model, including how ride sourcing services like Uber and Lyft are beginning to integrate their business with bike share service providers.
- Public reaction to bike share.
- Bike share gone wrong, looking at systems that have failed to achieve their ridership estimates.
- The future of bike share including public transport smart card integration, mobile payments and electric assist bicycles.

The book provides scholars, city planners, transportation practitioners and students with a resource that captures the most pertinent scientific findings and practical lessons that have been from bike share programs around the world.

Elliot Fishman is a transport researcher and consultant who has specialised in bicycle planning and disruptive transport innovation for over a decade. He completed his PhD on bike share and has advised the OECD, the Australian Prime Minister's Office and numerous government agencies on transport innovation and continues to work as a transport consultant as Director of the Institute for Sensible Transport.

Bike Share

Elliot Fishman

Routledge
Taylor & Francis Group
NEW YORK AND LONDON

First published 2020
by Routledge
52 Vanderbilt Avenue, New York, NY 10017

and by Routledge
2 Park Square, Milton Park, Abingdon, Oxon, OX14 4RN

Routledge is an imprint of the Taylor & Francis Group, an informa business

© 2020 Taylor & Francis

Library of Congress Cataloging-in-Publication Data
Names: Fishman, Elliot, 1976– author.
Title: Bike share / Elliot Fishman.
Description: New York, NY: Routledge, 2020.
Identifiers: LCCN 2019014623 (print) | LCCN 2019021746 (ebook) | ISBN 9781315545127 (e-book) | ISBN 9781138682481 (hardback) | ISBN 9781138682498 (pbk.)
Subjects: LCSH: Bicycle sharing programs.
Classification: LCC HE5736 (ebook) | LCC HE5736 .F46 2020 (print) | DDC 388.3/472—dc23
LC record available at https://lccn.loc.gov/2019014623

ISBN: 978-1-138-68248-1 (hbk)
ISBN: 978-1-138-68249-8 (pbk)
ISBN: 978-1-315-54512-7 (ebk)

Typeset in Bembo
by codeMantra

Printed and bound by CPI Group (UK) Ltd, Croydon, CR0 4YY

Contents

Acknowledgements

There are a number of people that provided invaluable assistance in the development of this book. First, I need to thank Associate Professor Matthew Burke, whose wise recommendation in 2010 to ask Professor Simon Washington to be my PhD supervisor has had a lasting influence on my research direction. It was Professor Washington who suggested bike share might be an interesting topic for a PhD. Professor Narelle Haworth, as my Associate Supervisor during my PhD at the Centre for Accident Research and Road Safety – Queensland was a constant source of wise and strategic advice that enhanced the quality of my research. This book would not have been possible without the support offered by Professors Washington and Haworth.

I would like to thank Russell Meddin and Paul DeMaio of the Bike Share blogspot, both of whom are a reliable source of information on bike share around the world. Many of the tables and figures in this book are the result of data provided by Russell.

During this book's development, I have spoken to many bike share operators and suppliers. They have been very generous with their time and sharing their insights into the commercial and operational aspects of bike share.

I am also incredibly grateful to Liam Davies and Vaughn Allan, two of my colleagues at the Institute for Sensible Transport. Their assistance at various times throughout the development of this book has been very useful.

Finally, I would like to thank my wife, Meredith, who has put up with a lot of single parenting to enable me to complete this book.

1 Introduction

The year 2007 marked a monumental shift in the evolution of human settlement. For the first time in human history, more than 50% of the world's population lived in cities (World Health Organization, 2010), and this trend is set to see this grow to 70% by 2050. Commentators have described the current epoch as the *Urban Age*, characterised by a service-led economy where cities are the economic powerhouse of nations, responsible for a growing proportion of the population and GDP. The focus of this book is bike share, but prior to addressing the myriad of topics within this burgeoning new mobility option, it is necessary to contextualise bike share within wider transformations in urban transport. The changes brought about in the decades following the Second World War act as the foundation upon which 'transport alternatives', such as bike share began to emerge.

As urban populations have grown upwards and outwards, in combination with increasingly attainable motor vehicles, transport systems have come under unprecedented strain. The growth in motor vehicle ownership continues to grow, even though there is some evidence that per capita car usage is beginning to reduce in some developed countries (Goodwin & Van Dender, 2013).

Bike share is inextricably linked with the emergence of the sharing economy generally. What was once a relatively stagnant set of transport choices in cities has now seen a widening of options that include App-based ride sourcing platforms (e.g., Uber, Didi), peer-2-peer car share (e.g., Snappcar, Getaround), and on demand, App-based public transport. To a greater or lesser extent, these non-traditional forms of transport have diversified mobility options in cities, which have the potential to reduce car ownership (Shaheen & Cohen, 2018). These developments are now categorised as Mobility as a Service (MaaS) and also include the burgeoning shared e-scooter sector,[1] which has rapidly developed in North America during the 2017–2019 period, with many other markets beginning to see e-scooters emerge as an additional transport option.

Business models are changing as well, with traditional vehicle manufacturers buying large stakes in ride sourcing service companies (e.g., GM investing $500 million in Lyft) and ride sourcing service companies buying up bike share companies (e.g., Lyft buying Motivate, the largest bike share company in the United States). In April 2018, Uber acquired JUMP, the NYC-based bike share company that operates electric bike share in San Francisco, Washington, D.C., and a number of other cities. The key value proposition for cities and communities from these platforms is that they offer mobility without the need for ownership. This helps to grow transport choices and can encourage a more rational use of the car.

1.1 Car Dependence

The urban environment was radically transformed in most developed world cities in the decades following the end of the Second World War, to accommodate the insatiable space requirements of large-scale motorised transport. The space efficiency rating of different modes of transport is shown in Figure 1.1. It shows that a 3.5 m lane can carry 2,000 people by car[2] per hour, 9,000 by bus and 14,000 by bicycle. Whilst public transport is most efficient in this regard, the bicycle is the most efficient vehicle that can be used individually, without adherence to a timetable.

The effort cities across the globe went to in an attempt to accommodate the space requirements of the car have been catalogued elsewhere (e.g., see Givoni & Banister, 2010; Hickman & Banister, 2014; Newman & Kenworthy, 1999). Needless to say, these efforts have been among the largest reallocation of public space in the modern history of cities. Town squares, riverbanks, oceanfronts and forest have all given way to the space

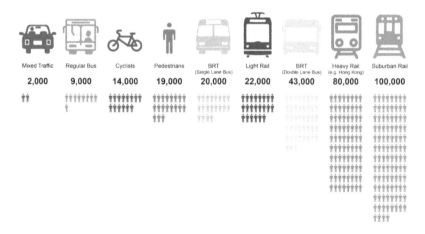

Figure 1.1 Carrying capacity of different modes, 3.5 m carriageway.
Source: United Nations (2013).

requirements of large-scale car use. Approximately half of urban land is paved to facilitate mass car use (in Los Angles this rises to 61%) according to Manville and Shoup (2005).

Car-based urban transport mentalities have, over decades, resulted in what transport researchers Professors Newman and Kenworthy coined *automobile dependence* (Newman & Kenworthy, 1999), in which the travel choices people make became constrained as spending on urban freeways grew and public transport investment decreased. The broadening geography of cities made the automobile the *default* mode for many, and this had a self-reinforcing circle that Ivan Illich captures succinctly in the passage below taken from *Energy and Equity* (Illich, 1973):

> Beyond a certain speed, motorized vehicles create remoteness which they alone can shrink. They create distances for all and shrink them for only a few.

The cycle of car dependence is illustrated in Figure 1.2.

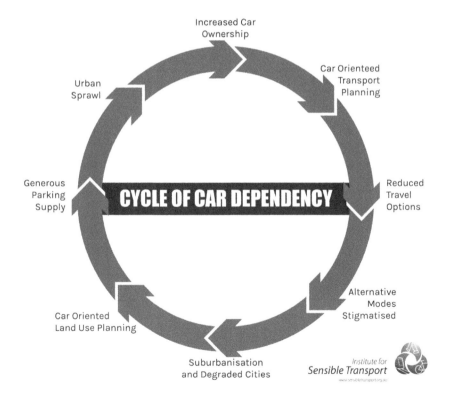

Figure 1.2 Cycle of car dependence.
Source: Litman (2016).

The *Cycle of Car Dependency* illustrated in Figure 1.2 is particularly prevalent in the outer suburbs of North American and Australian cities, in which almost all trips are driven, often with an occupancy rate of around 1.1 people per vehicle. This phenomenon has been termed *forced car use* by Professor Graham Currie et al. (2007), where people must drive, regardless of what their preference might be, as it is the only viable mode of transport on offer. Figure 1.3 provides an illustration of mode share across a range of cities. Melbourne, Los Angeles and Sydney all show the car accounts for more than half of all trips. Berlin, Beijing and Shanghai demonstrate a more diversified mix of transport modes, with no single mode type making up more than 35% of all trips.

It is important to recognise that for all the cities shown in Figure 1.3 (with the exception of Beijing and Shanghai), the data relate to the *journey to work*. However, whilst it is common to focus on this journey type, in reality, it constitutes only a small percentage of overall travel (usually between 15% and 20% of all trips). Figure 1.4 provides a snapshot of journey types for Paris and London, demonstrating that the commute represents a minority of trips. Importantly, non-work trips tend to be of shorter distance and duration than commute trips (Transport for NSW, 2014). This is important as it is the trips between 1 and 7 km that are most easily transferred to bike share, as longer trips become uncompetitive with motorised transport.

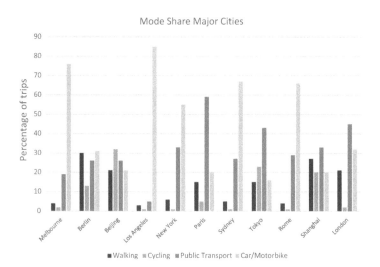

Figure 1.3 Mode share, selected cities.
Source: Australian Bureau of Statistics (2017), DRIEA (2013), EPOMM (n.d.), PASTA (n.d.), Transport for London (2017), and United States Census Bureau (2013).
NB: Rome: 'Car' also includes other forms of private motorised transport, including scooters/mopeds.

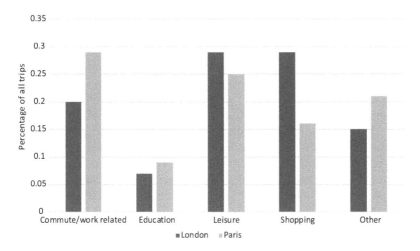

Figure 1.4 Journey purpose, London and Paris.
Source: London data from Transport for London (2012) with some categories collapsed to enable comparison with Paris. Paris data from Île-de-France Region (2013).

One possible reason for the rise in the popularity of bike share is the high number of trips occurring in cities that are within a cyclable distance. For instance, in Sydney, over 6 million *car* trips currently take place on an average weekday that are under 5 km, according to the Sydney Household Travel Survey (Transport for NSW, 2014). Similarly, in London, a third of car trips are less than 2 km (Transport for London, 2012). This underlines the potential for bike share to act as an effective replacement for the millions of short car trips taking place in the world's major cities every day. Conventional understandings of transport mode choice recognise that travel choice is a balance between time competitiveness, cost and convenience (Schwanen & Mokhtarian, 2005). Interestingly, there is also some evidence that *difficulty finding a car park* can be a central motivation for using non-car-based transport options (Transport for NSW, 2014). This underlines a central theme within this book; *people do not make transport decisions in isolation.* They consider the pros and cons of the various modes available. Bike share, if it is to be well used, needs to be competitive on a time, cost and convenience basis. It also needs to feel safe, and a lack of bike infrastructure is a principle barrier to higher levels of cycling in many cities (Pucher & Buehler, 2011, 2012).

More recently, the public transport planner Jarrett Walker has outlined some of the simple rules of geometry that make widespread car use unsuitable for growing cities (Walker, 2016). Walker explains that as a city's population grows faster than the land area it consumes, there is less space per person, and because cars take up a lot of space, congestion is the inevitable consequence of a policy fixated on maintaining current levels of car use. As Walker said recently, 'if it doesn't scale, it doesn't matter' (Walker, 2018), meaning that if a certain mode of transport does not effectively move large volumes of people in a space-efficient manner, it is not a mode of transport suitable for densifying cities.

Autonomous vehicles are anticipated by some to become a reality on city streets over the next 5–15 years. Already, a large number of companies are testing driverless cars on public streets. In 2018, Waymo, the computer-driven car unit of Google parent company 'Alphabet', was given approval to test cars without a safety/backup driver on public roads in California. These driverless cars are likely to open up affordable 'robo-taxis' that whilst potentially improving road safety could exacerbate car use and congestion (Fagnant & Kockelman, 2015). People too old or young to drive cars may be able to summon them in the future. The cost of e-hailing a robo taxi could be equivalent to a public transport ticket, encouraging more people to opt for the door-to-door convenience of car use over the more space-efficient public transport service. People may also choose to live further away from their work, as they no longer have to engage in the act of driving, freeing them to do other things. Some researchers also speculate that driverless cars (especially if privately owned) may contribute to the so-called 'empty miles' where a car without any occupants is summoned to make a pickup. All these scenarios are plausible and result in greater vehicle kilometres travelled (VKT).

1.2 Individually Owned Cars Were Never a Good Match for Cities

Cars and cities were never a good match. A car is the second most expensive item most people will ever buy, yet they sit unused for 96% of the day (Shoup, 2005). Each motor vehicle requires between four and eight car parking spots, and the cost of providing these spaces drives up the cost of everything else, including housing (Shoup, 2005).

Over 30,000 people die each year due to motor vehicle crashes in the United States alone (over 1,300,000 globally), and more people die globally in road trauma than due to malaria (by a factor of three). As the former New York City Transportation Commissioner Janet Sadik-Khan writes, 'Transportation is one of the few professions where nearly 30,000 people can lose their lives in one year and no one in a position of responsibility is in danger of losing his or her job' (Sadik-Khan & Solomonow, 2016, p. 29).

By any measure, the transport system responsible for the negative impacts described above has reached its use-by date. These issues have been recognised for some time (Newman & Kenworthy, 1999), and virtually all large cities in OECD nations have transport strategies ostensibly intended to offer alternatives to private motor vehicle use. Breaking the *Cycle of Car Dependence* has proved difficult, and few examples exist in which changes in transport policy have led to substantially lower car use and a rise in sustainable mobility.[3] Very often, where a significant lowering in car dependence has arisen, it is at least in part due to an external event, such as a fuel crisis[4] (e.g., Cuba in the early 1990s or the Netherlands in 1973) or contraction in economic growth.

The widely acknowledged problems associated with large-scale car ownership and dependence, coupled with social and technological change, opens a new chapter in the history of urban transport, and bike share is emerging as an important element within this story of *new urban mobility*.

1.3 The Bicycle's Place in the New Urban Mobility Agenda

The grip of automobile dependence has begun to show signs of weakening, with a widespread, albeit relatively modest trend recorded of reduced per capita car ownership and use (Stapleton, Sorrell, & Schwanen, 2017). Whilst it is too early to know precisely which factors are causing this global, somewhat slow shift away from car use in some countries, the trend is surprisingly widespread among developed countries. A combination of changing attitudes, demographics, lifestyle preferences and technology is cited as the contributing factor to the shift away from automobile-dependent lifestyles (Hoffmann, Kandt, Smith, & Graff, 2015). A growing awareness of the importance of *liveability* has led to an emerging recalibration of city life, in which the car's long-held position as the centrepiece of people's mobility options is beginning to change.

A recent Special Issue of *The Lancet* was dedicated to the benefits of moving away from automobile-dependent transport planning (e.g., see Giles-Corti et al., 2016; Sallis et al., 2016; Stevenson et al., 2016). The bicycle, owing to its positive impact on physical activity, air quality, climate change combined with its space efficiency and affordability, has emerged as a critical element of this *new urban mobility*.

The prospect of social and commercial *interaction* attracted people to cities several thousand years ago, and the bicycle has found itself as a very useful tool to facilitate this most basic of human needs (Fishman, 2016). As Illich notes, 'only the bicycle really allows people to go from door to door without walking' (1973, p. 62), and it is this unique attribute that has helped to refocus the attention of city and transport planners to the role the bicycle is able to play in urban areas. Ultimately of course, it cannot and should not be 'about the bike', but rather on the benefits the bicycle brings to cities, in the form of carbon-free, healthy, low-cost and space-efficient mobility. Cities that are bicycle friendly are more likely to be productive, attractive cities. Copenhagen and Amsterdam are certainly much more frequently mentioned as desirable cities in which to visit than cities where 85%–90% of all trips are done by car. As more cities begin to recognise the benefits cycling offers, bike share has become an increasingly popular method of enhancing transport choice, urban productivity and sustainability.

1.4 Bike Share in the Context of Transport Systems

One useful method of thinking about bike share (and other modes of transport for that matter) is by isolating the three fundamental elements that each mode of transport holds. The UCLA Professor, best known for his work on parking policy, Donald Shoup has identified that each mode of transport consists of three elements; the vehicle, rights of way and terminal capacity (Shoup 2010).

Each mode of transport typically requires these three elements (with the exception of walking). Maritime transport, for example, requires ships (the vehicle), shipping lanes (rights of way) and ports (terminal capacity).

For bicycling, the vehicles are *bicycles*, the rights of way are *streets* and *bicycle paths*, and terminal capacity is *bicycle racks* or similar devices to lock bicycles. 'Traditional' bike share programs address two of these three elements, namely, they provide the *vehicle* (bicycle) and the *terminal capacity* (docking station). Dockless bike share, which will be discussed throughout this book (e.g., Section 6.2 and Chapter 7), only provide the *vehicle*, with city governments required to provide the terminal capacity (bicycle parking), in addition to sufficient *rights of way* (bike lanes and paths). Failing to provide sufficient *rights of way* (e.g., protected bicycle lanes) can act as a barrier to bike share use, as will be described in Chapter 9.

The role of government and the private sector varies in contributing to these three elements, depending on the mode of transport in question. Some bike share services are entirely government owned, with the public sector owning the docking stations (terminal capacity), bicycles (vehicle) and streets (rights of way) entirely held by the government. However, increasingly, the vehicle (bicycle) is being provided by the commercial sector, and the need for docking stations reduced through the emergence of GPS-connected, self-locking bikes. Even in fully commercial bike share, there will always be a reliance on public-sector infrastructure, both for terminal capacity space (parking the bike) and for the rights of way (e.g., bike lanes and paths).

Importantly, bike share is seen as a *first mile/last mile* solution (Shaheen, Guzman, & Zhang, 2010), helping to improve access to and from public transport (Parkes, Marsden, Shaheen, & Cohen, 2013). The integration of cycling and public transport is said to make up for the weakness of both. When planned to complement each other, over 40% of train journeys can start with a bicycle trip, as has been demonstrated in the Netherlands (Ministerie van Verkeer en Waterstaat, 2009). A bike share network designed to act as a feeder to public transport can substantially enhance the functional catchment of public transport. See Chapter 11 for additional information on integrating bike share with public transport.

This book documents bike share's place within the context of cities seeking to lower car use and increase the vibrancy and productivity of urban life. The book provides scholars, city planners, transportation practitioners and students with a resource that captures the most pertinent scientific findings and practical lessons that have been from bike share programs around the world.

Notes

1 E-scooters are not the focus of this book as they do not have pedals and therefore not considered a bicycle.
2 At average peak hour occupancies of around 1.2 people per vehicle.
3 Thankfully there are some notable exceptions to this, such as almost every city in the Netherlands, as well as Copenhagen, Denmark.
4 The Netherlands shift towards sustainable mobility was not entirely voluntary. The 1973 oil embargo, and a spike in road traffic fatalities involving children also spurred the Dutch interest in sustainable transport options.

References

Australian Bureau of Statistics. (2017). Census 2016 from Australian Government. Retrieved from http://www.abs.gov.au/websitedbs/censushome.nsf/home/2016
Currie, G., Stanley, J., & Stanley, J. (2007). *No Way to Go: Transport and Social Disadvantage in Australian communities*. Melbourne: Monash University ePress.
DRIEA. (2013). Enquête globale transport; La mobilité en Île-de-France. Retrieved from http://www.driea.ile-de-france.developpement-durable.gouv.fr/enquete-globale-de-transport-r18.html
EPOMM. (n.d.). TEMS – The EPOMM Modal Split Tool. Retrieved from http://www.epomm.eu/tems/index.phtml
Fagnant, D. J., & Kockelman, K. (2015). Preparing a nation for autonomous vehicles: Opportunities, barriers and policy recommendations. *Transportation Research Part A: Policy and Practice, 77*, 167–181. doi:10.1016/j.tra.2015.04.003
Fishman, E. (2016). Cycling as transport. *Transport Reviews, 36*(1), 1–8. doi:10.1080/01441647.2015.1114271
Giles-Corti, B., Vernez-Moudon, A., Reis, R., Turrell, G., Dannenberg, A. L., Badland, H., … Owen, N. (2016). City planning and population health: A global challenge. *The Lancet*. doi:10.1016/S0140-6736(16)30066-6
Givoni, M., & Banister, D. (2010). *Integrated Transport from Policy to Practice*. Hoboken, NJ: Taylor & Francis.
Goodwin, P., & Van Dender, K. (2013). 'Peak car' – Themes and issues. *Transport Reviews, 33*(3), 243–254. doi:10.1080/01441647.2013.804133
Hickman, R., & Banister, D. (2014). *Transport, Climate Change and the City*. London: Routledge.
Hoffmann, C., Kandt, J., Smith, D., & Graff, A. (2015). Toward New Urban Mobility: The Case of London and Berlin. Retrieved from London: https://files.lsecities.net/files/2015/09/New-Urban-Mobility-London-and-Berlin.pdf
Île-de-France Region. (2013). La mobilité en Île-de-France. Retrieved from http://www.driea.ile-de-france.developpement-durable.gouv.fr/IMG/pdf/Fiche_Paris_BD_cle5316c5.pdf
Illich, I. (1973). *Energy and Equity*. New York: Harper & Row.
Litman, T. (2016). Automobile Dependency. Retrieved from http://www.vtpi.org/tdm/tdm100.htm

Manville, M., & Shoup, D. (2005). Parking, people and cities. *Journal of Urban Planning and Development.* doi:10.1061/ASCE0733-94882005131:4233

Ministerie van Verkeer en Waterstaat. (2009). Cycling in the Netherlands. Retrieved from http://www.fietsberaad.nl/library/repository/bestanden/CyclingintheNetherlands2009.pdf

Newman, P., & Kenworthy, J. (1999). *Sustainability and Cities: Overcoming Automobile Dependence.* Washington, DC: Island Press.

Parkes, S. D., Marsden, G., Shaheen, S. A., & Cohen, A. P. (2013). Understanding the diffusion of public bikesharing systems: Evidence from Europe and North America. *Journal of Transport Geography, 31,* 94–103.

PASTA. (n.d.). Facts on Active Mobility Rome, Italy. Retrieved from Rome: http://www.pastaproject.eu/fileadmin/editor-upload/sitecontent/Publications/documents/AM_Factsheet_Rome_WP2.pdf

Pucher, J., & Buehler, R. (2011). Analysis of Bicycling Trends and Policies in Large North American Cities: Lessons for New York. Retrieved from https://trid.trb.org/view/1104384.

Pucher, J., & Buehler, R. (2012). *City Cycling.* Cambridge, MA: MIT Press.

Sadik-Khan, J., & Solomonow, S. (2016). *Streetfight: Handbook for an Urban Revolution.* New York: Viking.

Sallis, J. F., Bull, F., Burdett, R., Frank, L. D., Griffiths, P., Giles-Corti, B., & Stevenson, M. (2016). Use of science to guide city planning policy and practice: How to achieve healthy and sustainable future cities. *The Lancet.* doi:10.1016/S0140-6736(16)30068-X

Schwanen, T., & Mokhtarian, P. L. (2005). What affects commute mode choice: Neighborhood physical structure or preferences toward neighborhoods? *Journal of Transport Geography, 13,* 83–99. doi:10.1016/j.jtrangeo.2004.11.001

Shaheen, S., & Cohen, A. (2018). Shared ride services in North America: definitions, impacts, and the future of pooling. *Transport Reviews,* 427–442. doi.org/10.1080/01441647.2018.1497728

Shaheen, S., Guzman, S., & Zhang, H. (2010). Bikesharing in Europe, the Americas, and Asia. *Transportation Research Record: Journal of the Transportation Research Board, 2143,* 159–167. doi:10.3141/2143-20

Shoup, D. (2005). *The High Cost of Free Parking.* Chicago, IL: Planners Press.

Shoup, D. (2010). *The high cost of free parking: Key note address.* Paper presented at the The High Cost of Free Parking Seminar, Melbourne Town Hall. Retrieved from http://sensibletransport.org.au/project/the-high-cost-of-free-parking-seminar-with-professor-donald-shoup/

Stapleton, L., Sorrell, S., & Schwanen, T. (2017). Peak car and increasing rebound: A closer look at car travel trends in Great Britain. *Transportation Research Part D: Transport and Environment, 53,* 217–233.

Stevenson, M., Thompson, J., de Sá, T. H., Ewing, R., Mohan, D., McClure, R., … Woodcock, J. (2016). Land use, transport, and population health: Estimating the health benefits of compact cities. *The Lancet.* doi:10.1016/S0140-6736(16)30067-8

Transport for London. (2012). Roads Task Force – Technical Note 14 Who Travels by Car in London and for What Purpose? Retrieved from London: http://content.tfl.gov.uk/technical-note-14-who-travels-by-car-in-london.pdf

Transport for London. (2017). Travel in London: Report 10. Retrieved from London: http://content.tfl.gov.uk/travel-in-london-report-10.pdf

Transport for NSW. (2014). Household Travel Survey Report: Sydney 2012/13. Retrieved from Sydney: https://www.transport.nsw.gov.au/sites/default/files/media/documents/2017/HTS%20Report%20Sydney%202012-13.pdf

United Nations. (2013). Review of Developments in Transport in Asia and the Pacific. Retrieved from http://www.unescap.org/sites/default/files/Transport-Review_2013_full_text.pdf

United States Census Bureau. (2013). State and Country QuickFacts. Retrieved from http://quickfacts.census.gov/qfd/states/11000.html

Walker, J. (Producer). (2016). Why Cars and Cities Are a Bad Match [Opinion piece]. Retrieved from https://www.washingtonpost.com/news/in-theory/wp/2016/03/02/buses-and-trains-thats-what-will-solve-congestion/

Walker, J. (2018). Elon Musk's Tunnel: It Doesn't Scale, So It Doesn't Matter. Retrieved from https://humantransit.org/2018/12/elon-musks-tunnel-it-doesnt-scale-so-it-doesnt-matter.html

World Health Organization. (2010). Hidden Cities: Unmasking and Overcoming Health Inequalities in Urban Settings. Retrieved from http://www.who.int/kobe_centre/publications/hiddencities_media/who_un_habitat_hidden_cities_web.pdf?ua=1

2   Bike Share's History

Bike share has had a chequered history in the half century since the first 'program', known as *Witte Fietsen* ('White Bikes' in Dutch) was launched on the streets of Amsterdam in 1965. Although frequently referred to as the first *Bike Share Program*, it was in fact little more than a political stunt by the prominent activist group *Provo* (as in to *provoke*). Luud Schimmelpennink, a member of Provo at the time, is largely credited as the brainchild behind the concept of bike share. In fact, Schimmelpennink should be heralded as one of the fathers of *shared transport* in general, as he was also instrumental in the launch of one of the world's first electric car share programs.[1]

Witte Fietsen consisted of little more than five to ten bicycles, hand painted white, and left on the street for people to use freely (Schimmelpennink, 2014). The total absence of any security mechanisms led to theft and vandalism, and the rapid demise of the 'program' (DeMaio, 2009). Figure 2.1 shows the demonstrations held by Provo, promoting the concept of the Witte Fietsen Plan. Provo sought the support of Amsterdam City Council, in order to provide the scale necessary to have a meaningful impact on improving the city. The Council chose not to support Witte Fietsen and several attempts (successful and otherwise) by its originator, Schimmelpennink, to run for Council failed to attract municipal support for bike share.

Whilst Witte Fietsen was short lived, the concept of bike share had been born. The theft and vandalism that led to the demise of Witte Fietsen meant that bike share made little progress in the years immediately following Amsterdam's experiment. It was not until technological advancements enabled affordable security mechanisms to be added to the bicycles that other cities began to embark on bike share programs of their own.

Over half a century after the launch of Amsterdam's *White Bikes* demonstration, the city is still without a formalised bike share program (though no shortage of private bicycles exists) and Schimmelpennink, now in his 80s, is still advocating for one. In the summer of 2017, a number of dockless bike share firms launched in Amsterdam (without the consent of Amsterdam City Council), but these were short lived and removed only a few months after launch. At the time of writing, bike share's place within Amsterdam remains uncertain.

La Rochelle, France was quite possibly the first city to create a government authorised bike share program. In 1976, this seaside city of 75,000

Figure 2.1 White Bike program in Amsterdam, mid-1960s.
Source: Luud Schimmelpennink.

inhabitants introduced 250 bicycles, partly due to the increasing recognition of the need to encourage ecological forms of mobility (Hure & Passalacqua, 2017). Bicycle mode share had been declining for decades, both in France and other European countries, whilst car ownership had become much more widespread. The introduction of the La Rochelle bike share program was a political action to try and reassert low impact forms of mobility within this medium-sized French city. Interestingly, rather than a door-to-door form of transport, the bike share program was initially conceived as a kind of 'park and ride' initiative in an attempt to encourage motorists to park on the outskirts of the city and make the final leg of the journey on the *auto-velos* as the bikes were originally called, meaning *car-bikes* (Hure & Passalacqua, 2017). The bikes were intended to be free for everyone to use and in fact were inspired by the *shopping trolley*; in that they were available to be freely shared between people according to need. The bicycles were restricted to the inner urban core (though this was immediately and widely ignored) and consisted of 23 stations (Hure & Passalacqua, 2017). Due, in part, to the limited availability of security technology, the bicycles had to be picked up and stored overnight, meaning the system was only available during the day.

The La Rochelle system was financed through the State (60%) in combination with the City government (40%). Like more recent bike share systems, La Rochelle needed to renew its bicycles not long after launching (they opted for more sturdy bikes), and the catchment of the system needed to expand, as there were key destinations outside the original boundaries of the system (e.g., train station, beach). The system had ended but was relaunched in 2009 and now consists of around 300 bicycles, integrated with public transport.

The first bike share program in the United States started in the mid-1990s, via the actions of a small group of Portland, Oregon residents. The Portland group had become inspired by the story of *Witte Fietsen* and established *Yellow Bike*. Starting with 15 bicycles, and expanding to around 200, the project used donated, second-hand bikes, painted yellow. To reduce the ability of users to take the bicycles up hill and outside of the intended catchment, mechanics converted the bicycles to single speed. This grass roots program ultimately failed due to theft and vandalism and was disbanded 3 years after it began (Rose, 2016). One of the key lessons from the early experience with bike share is that despite the best of intentions, low-tech programs that rely on volunteers and the good will of citizens to use the bicycles as intended, generally fail. People steal and vandalize the bicycles, and managing the program and its fleet of bicycles often proven more difficult than envisioned. The rest of this chapter describes the evolution of bike share, from these low-tech experiments through to sophisticated, Internet-connected fleets of bicycles that can number in their millions in some cities (e.g., Beijing).

2.1 Evolution of Bike Share

Some researchers have categorised the evolution of bike share systems into four 'generations' (Parkes, Marsden, Shaheen, & Cohen, 2013). *White Bikes* described above is known as a *first-generation* bike share 'system', characterised by no payment or security functions. *Second-generation* programs involved a coin deposit system (similar to trolleys at a supermarket or airport). The first large-scale second-generation program launched in Copenhagen in 1995, but the anonymity also exposed the system to theft/vandalism (DeMaio, 2009) as it is easy to use a coin-operated system improperly. Ultimately a bike is worth more than a coin, and the anonymity of the user fails to deter those seeking to use the bikes outside their intended purpose.

The problems experienced by these first two generations of bike share led to the development of *third-generation* systems, which are characterised by dedicated docking stations (in which bicycles are picked up and returned), as well as automated credit card payment and other technologies to allow the tracking of the bicycles (Shaheen, Cohen, & Martin, 2013). It is these elements, in combination with growing public policy interest in cycling (Pucher & Buehler, 2012), that have enabled the rapid growth of bike share programs globally (Fishman, 2015). Up until 2016, almost all of the bike share programs established since 2005 could be classed as *third generation*. The features of *fourth-generation* systems are not quite so clear but are said to potentially include dockless systems, easier installation, electric assistance, and transit smartcard integration (Parkes et al., 2013). This book treats dockless bike share as fourth generation.

The bike share sector is currently in a state of flux; new technologies and business models have caused city governments to re-think public investment in bike share. As of late 2018, the commercial sector continues to demonstrate an enthusiasm for launching and managing bike share services without public subsidy. As to how this might influence the evolution of bike share is unclear. One of the trends evident in many North American cities, as well as a growing number of cities around the globe, is the emergence of e-scooters, and it is uncertain what impact the growth of e-scooters may have on bike share evolution. Early data have shown that the introduction of e-scooters coincided with record ridership of the existing docked bike share program. For example in Brisbane, Australia have had their highest bike share usage in the month e-scooters launched, whilst other cities have seen e-scooters cannibalise bike share usage. As tech companies and traditional vehicle manufacturers merge and acquire bike share firms, how bike share may evolve in the next decade is difficult to determine.

Note

1 Witkar was launched in Amsterdam in 1974 and ran for 12 years, with a peak membership of around 4,000.

References

DeMaio, P. (2009). Bike-sharing: History, impacts, models of provision, & future. *Journal of Public Transportation, 12*(4), 41–56.

Fishman, E. (2015). Bikeshare: A review of recent literature. *Transport Reviews*, 1–22. doi:10.1080/01441647.2015.1033036

Hure, M., & Passalacqua, A. (2017). La Rochelle, France, and the invention of bike sharing public policy in the 1970. *The Journal of Transport History, 38*(1), 106–123.

Parkes, S. D., Marsden, G., Shaheen, S. A., & Cohen, A. P. (2013). Understanding the diffusion of public bikesharing systems: Evidence from Europe and North America. *Journal of Transport Geography, 31*, 94–103.

Pucher, J., & Buehler, R. (2012). *City Cycling*. Cambridge, MA: MIT Press.

Rose, J. (2016). Remembering Portland's Disastrous Yellow Bike Project (Photos). Retrieved from https://www.oregonlive.com/history/2016/01/portlands_disastrous_yellow_bi.html

Schimmelpennink, L. (2014, 30th December). *Dutch Transport Innovation/Interviewer: E. Fishman*. Amsterdam: Institute for Sensible Transport.

Shaheen, S., Cohen, A. P., & Martin, E. W. (2013). Public bikesharing in North America: Early operator understanding and emerging trends. *Transportation Research Record: Journal of the Transportation Research Board, 2387*, 83–92. doi:10.3141/2387-10

3   The Growth of Bike Share

In the past decade, the number of cities operating bike share programs has increased from 13 in 2004 to over 1,300 cities as of 2018. There are now over 2,130 individual bike share programs, with many cities having multiple bike share programs (Meddin, 2018). As shown in Figure 3.1, the global growth in bike share began around 2005–2007. It was during this period that two French cities launched relatively large schemes that used street advertising contracts as a method of paying for bike share. Lyon and Paris launched their bike share programs in 2005 and 2007, respectively, and Paris in particular attracted a great deal of public attention, owing to both its status as an international city and the sheer size of the program (~20,000 bikes). Many Mayors and other city officials from around the globe travelled to Paris and decided their city too should have a bike share program. In this sense, Paris became the inspiration for bike share's rapid global growth.

As of December 2018, it is estimated there are now over 20 million bike share bikes, with the overwhelming majority of them being *dockless*.

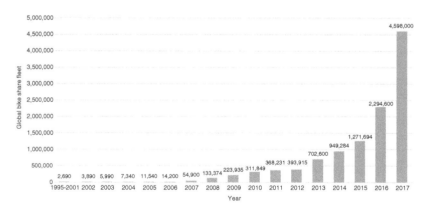

Figure 3.1 Bike share's global fleet size (number of bikes), 2017.
Source: R. Meddin, personal communication – Bike share global numbers (2017).
NB: Numbers are indicative only, as there is uncertainty particularly of dockless bike share numbers, as these are privately held companies and it is not always clear how many are actually on the street at any one time.

It is now becoming increasingly difficult to determine the number of bicycles within bike share systems, as there are multiple commercial suppliers that are placing bicycles in the same city, competing with one another, often without any formal government involvement. Some have drawn comparisons to *Uber*, the App-based ride hailing service which often entered markets without any formal authorisation. Dockless bike share is covered in Chapter 7. Table 3.1 provides a selection of cities with bike share programs, highlighting the type of bike share offered (dockless, docked or hybrid), as well as the number of bicycles. It clearly shows the dominance of large Chinese cities, with fleets of over hundreds of thousands of bikes, and in the case of Beijing and Shanghai, millions.

The United States, a relative latecomer to bike share, has seen a rapid increase in the number of cities offering bike share. It is estimated that the total number of bike share bikes in the United States rose from 42,500 by the end of 2016 to around 100,000 just 12 months later, with ridership growing by 25% (NACTO, 2018). In 2016, it was estimated riders took over 28 million trips using bike share in the United States (Institute for Transportation & Development Policy, 2018a). Several cities now include

Table 3.1 Bike share cities, type and size

City	Type	Number of bikes
Beijing	Dockless	2,000,000
Shanghai	Dockless	1,500,000
Guangzhou	Dockless	800,000
Tianjin	Dockless	300,000
Paris	Docked	24,500
London	Docked	20,439
Barcelona	Docked	10,240
New York City	Docked	9,789
Mexico City	Docked	6,500
Montreal	Docked	6,250
Chicago	Docked	5,800
Vancouver	Docked	5,493
Washington, D.C.	Docked	3,700
Buenos Aires	Docked	3,000
Cologne	Hybrid	2,500
Sydney	Dockless	2,000
Seattle	Dockless	1,908
Minneapolis	Docked	1,833
Brisbane	Docked	1,800
Portland	Hybrid	1,702
Dublin	Docked	1,600
Boulder	Docked	1,600
Milan	Docked	1,450
Atlanta	Hybrid	1,361
Rio de Janeiro	Docked	1,100
Melbourne	Docked	550

Source: Institute for Transportation & Development Policy (2018b).

a combination of docked and dockless bike share in the United States (e.g., San Francisco and Washington, D.C.).

Bike share is not restricted to wealthy countries/cities, and in fact, most of the world's bike share bikes are located in developing countries. China in particular stands out with a large number of cities successfully integrating bike share (docked or dockless) into their transport system. Dockless, in particular, has fuelled the growth of bike share in many parts of the world. Whilst the largest of these systems are in China, South America has seen the introduction of bike schemes with over 1,000 bicycles in Santiago, Chile and Buenos Aires, Argentina to name just two, Mexico City also has a well-used system with over 6,000 bikes, and Guadalajara has a system of almost 2,000 bikes. A handful of Indian cities have small-scale bike share programs, with Pune having the largest at 3,000 dockless bikes, making it the largest system in India by a considerable margin (Meddin, 2018).

3.1 Size Matters

Bike share systems can range from as little as 15 bikes, right through to giant Chinese systems with more than 1.9 million bikes (Beijing). The number of bikes in a bike share system is important because, as will be described later, bike share is a nodal system and its success is somewhat dependent on the number of nodes bicycles can be accessed and returned. As will be discussed in Chapter 11, the size of a bike share system can have an important impact on its usability. Though system size is not the only factor governing bike share success (e.g., see Médard de Chardon, Caruso, & Thomas, 2017), systems that are small relative to the size of the city in which it is located can have a detrimental impact on usage (Institute for Transportation & Development Policy, 2013, 2018a).

There can be a tendency for nervous officials to elect to go with a smaller system than the size of their city would suggest, out of fear the system may fail. If it does fail, so the reasoning goes, at least it may be seen as a 'small failure'. The problem with this rationale of course is that is can be a self-fulfilling prophecy, in which it fails *because* it was too small. The experience in Melbourne, Australia offers a good illustration of this, with only one bicycle for every 8,000 residents, well outside international standards of between 10 and 30 bikes per 1,000 residents for large dense cities (Institute for Transportation & Development Policy, 2013). Whilst Melbourne is large but not dense, a ratio of perhaps 2–5 bikes per 1,000 might have been more appropriate. Whilst fear of failure is one reason for cities to select to go with a small system, it must also be recognised that *cost* is also a critical determinant of how many bikes will be in a system. It often surprises city officials to learn that a typical cost for a docked system is around $US6,000–$US10,000 per bike, including docking infrastructure.

3.1.1 System Performance

The impacts of bike share are directly related to the degree to which it is used (Fishman, Washington, Haworth, & Watson, 2015; Shaheen, Martin, Chan, Cohen, & Pogodzinski, 2014). In comparing system usage between different cities, it has become standard to use the metric trips per day per bike, as this controls for variation in the number of bikes in a system. Figure 3.2 illustrates trips per day per bike for several prominent bike share programs for which the author was able to obtain the necessary data. It shows considerable differences in usage from almost 6 trips per day, per bike (Lyon), to as low as 0.3 trips per day, per bike (Brisbane).

Bike share programs are busier in the warmer months, which generally confirm the relationship between weather and propensity to cycle found in research on private bike riding (Ahmed, Rose, & Jacob, 2010). Of the cities included in Figure 3.2, Lyon and Barcelona are the most heavily used, with New York City's Citi Bike achieving a remarkably strong performance given its relatively severe winters. During summer, Citi Bike can achieve up to nine trips per bike per day. Washington, D.C., consistently reaches four to five trips per day per bike in summer, and even sometimes, icy winters have at least twice the usage of Australian bike share programs during their busiest months (January/February). Melbourne and Brisbane have around 0.8 and 0.3 trips per day per bike, respectively. The low usage level of Australian bike share programs will be examined in Chapter 9.

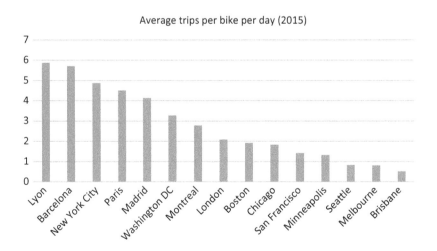

Figure 3.2 Bike share ridership, selected cities, 2015.
Source: Fishman (2015).

As one might expect, weekday bike share usage peaks between 7 am–9 am and 4 pm–6 pm, whilst weekend usage is strongest in the middle of the day (Pfrommer, Warrington, Schildbach, & Morari, 2013). Density is also an important determinant of bike share use. Figure 3.3 shows the relationship between density (people per hectare) and bike share use (trips per day, per bike). The data presented in Figure 3.3 can be used as a rough estimate of bike share's likely performance in cities that are yet to establish their program. It is of course important to recognise that density is just one explanatory factor for bike share performance. Bicycle infrastructure, difficulty of car use, density of docking stations and demographics will also influence the number of trips that take on a city's bike share system.

Cities with a low density will need to calibrate their expectations regarding bike share use. They are unlikely to experience usage levels within the 4–6 trips per day, per bike range, regardless of the quality of bicycles or other system design characteristics. The data presented in Figure 3.3 should act as reminder, for low-density cities, in particular, they will need to do everything in their control to maximise the attractiveness of using bike share. Meticulous attention to each of the factors known to boost usage levels that are amenable to intervention will be required to avoid the outcome of an under-used system. Creating a system that is under-used runs the risk of undermining future investment in cycling infrastructure and can consume scarce public funds.

Ultimately, systems that are too small for the city (low number of bikes per population is one metric) fail to provide the network coverage

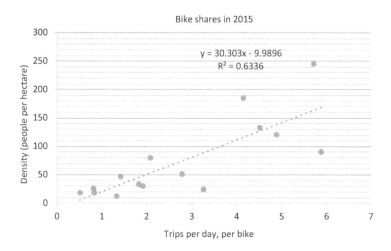

Figure 3.3 Density and bike share performance.
Source: Fishman (2017).

necessary to make bike share a viable mode of transport. This will be discussed in Chapter 9 when we look at the factors that contributed to the disappointing usage levels of the Melbourne Bike Share program.

References

Ahmed, F., Rose, G., & Jacob, C. (2010). *Impact of weather on commuter cyclist behaviour and implications for climate change adaptation.* Paper presented at the Australasian Transport Research Forum, Canberra.

Fishman, E. (2015). Bikeshare: A review of recent literature. *Transport Reviews,* 1–22. doi:10.1080/01441647.2015.1033036

Fishman, E. (2017). Canberra Bike Share: Initial Considerations. Retrieved from Melbourne: https://sensibletransport.org.au/project/canberra-bike-share/

Fishman, E., Washington, S., Haworth, N., & Watson, A. (2015). Factors influencing bike share membership: An analysis of Melbourne and Brisbane. *Transportation Research Part A, 71,* 17–30. doi:10.1016/j.tra.2014.10.021

Institute for Transportation & Development Policy. (2013). The Bike-sharing Planning Guide. Retrieved from New York: https://www.itdp.org/the-bike-share-planning-guide-2/

Institute for Transportation & Development Policy. (2018a). The Bikeshare Planning Guide. Retrieved from New York: https://www.itdp.org/publication/the-bike-share-planning-guide/

Institute for Transportation & Development Policy. (2018b). Bikeshare System Information & Performance Metrics. Retrieved from http://bikeshare.itdp.org/wp-content/uploads/2018/06/BIKESHARE_SystemInfoPerformance.pdf

Médard de Chardon, C., Caruso, G., & Thomas, I. (2017). Bicycle sharing system 'success' determinants. *Transportation Research Part A: Policy and Practice, 100,* 202–214.

Meddin, R. (2018). The Bike-sharing World Map. Retrieved from www.bikesharingmap.com

NACTO. (2018). Bike Share in the U.S. 2017. Retrieved from https://nacto.org/bike-share-statistics-2017/

Pfrommer, J., Warrington, J., Schildbach, G., & Morari, M. (2013). Dynamic vehicle redistribution and online price incentives in shared mobility systems. *arXiv preprint arXiv:1304.3949.* doi:10.1109/TITS.2014.2303986

Shaheen, S., Martin, E., Chan, N., Cohen, A., & Pogodzinski, M. (2014). *Public bikesharing in North America during a period of rapid expansion: Understanding business models, industry trends and user impacts, MTI* (Report No. CA-MTI-14-1131).

4 The Benefits of Bike Share

City governments have introduced bike share for the benefits they associate with increased urban cycling: improved population health, air and noise pollution reduction, and as a response to combating climate change. Added to these benefits are potential travel time savings, increased transport mode flexibility[1] and enhanced possibilities for integration with public transport (Fishman, 2015). There may also be some benefit that comes when bike share acts to transfer peak hour public transport journeys, as one seat freed up on a heavily loaded train is in essence a new seat made available for someone else.[2]

It is also apparent that bike share has become a symbol for elected officials seeking to brand their city as progressive, urbane and sustainable (Fishman, 2014). This was, of course, helped by the fact that Paris was one of the first OECD cities to establish a very large bike share program and that their program, *Velib*, is very heavily used (account for around 40% of all bicycle movements in Paris according to the operator JC Decaux). Cities seeking to attain status as an 'international city' may see bike share as one step towards that goal, especially given that so many cities that have prominent bike share programs (e.g., Paris, London, New York) are regarded as international cities.

This chapter examines available research evaluating the degree to which the purported benefits of bike share are being realised and concludes with some of the necessary, additional measures required to improve the ability of city agencies and researchers to evaluate the benefits of bike share.

4.1 Impacts on Motor Vehicle Use

Many of the most heavily promoted benefits of bike share (e.g., congestion reduction, climate change mitigation) are contingent on bike share being used as a replacement for motor vehicle travel (Fishman, 2014). Indeed, there is little to be gained from a climate change or congestion perspective when one uses bike share to replace a trip formally completed by foot or public transport (Médard de Chardon, Caruso, & Thomas, 2017). This, of course, has not stopped bike share operators from tallying up an estimate of the total number of kilometres travelled on their bike share fleet and then simply assuming *all* of that travel came as a direct replacement for motor vehicle travel. As will be outlined in this chapter, it is unlikely that a high proportion of bike share trips replace journeys previously completed by car. Thankfully, researchers and some city agencies have taken steps to remove the guess work that was becoming all too frequent in the early days of modern bike share (1998–2010).

An increasingly common question directed towards bike share users is 'For your last bike share trip, what mode of transport would you have used if bike share was not available?' The answer to this question is crucial to developing an understanding of the impact bike share has on transport sustainability and many of the other benefits of bike share identified above. A consistent theme has emerged when examining responses to this question; most of the trips are replacing trips formerly made by public transport and walking (Fishman, Washington, & Haworth, 2014). The results for a selected number of bike share cities are shown in Figure 4.1.

Some evaluation studies have asked bike share members whether the availability of bike share has influenced their car ownership. *Capital Bikeshare* in Washington, D.C. as part of its regular member survey found that 44% of members didn't have access to a car, and another 20% of respondents said that they reduced their driving, by an average of 1,565 miles per year, resulting in almost 10 million miles less driving (LDA Consulting, 2017). Members also reported using car services (e.g., Uber) less due to bike share (LDA Consulting, 2017). An earlier annual survey of *Capital Bikeshare* members found 5% of respondents reported selling a household vehicle since joining, and 80% of these members said bike share was a factor in their decision to sell the vehicle (LDA Consulting, 2013). It is remarkable how little research has examined the impact of bike share on car ownership, and the LDA Consulting research on *Capital Bikeshare* stands out as one of the new studies to look at this potentially important impact.

Another important consideration when determining the car use reduction benefits of bike share is the amount of *truck movements* bike share

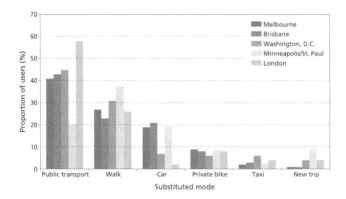

Figure 4.1 Mode being substituted by bike share in selected cities.
Source: Melbourne and Brisbane (Fishman, Washington, & Haworth, 2014), Washington, D.C. (LDA Consulting, 2012), Minnesota (Nice Ride Minnesota, 2010) and London (Transport for London, 2011a).

operators undertake to perform rebalancing. Rebalancing will be described in more detail in Box 8.2, but essentially, it refers to operator initiated movement of bicycles around the system when some areas become devoid of bikes, whilst other areas have too many. Fleet rebalancing is typically achieved through the use of trucks and trailers, and these are associated with many of the very impacts bike share aims to reduce (e.g. congestion, pollution).[3] An article published in the journal *Transportation Research Part D* (see Fishman, Washington, & Haworth, 2014) collected the necessary data to estimate the impact of bike share on car use, and these data are presented in Table 4.1 (using 2012 figures).

Table 4.1 demonstrates the impact *car substitution* has on *estimated car travel reduction*. Car travel reduction has been calculated by multiplying the estimated distance travelled by the car substitution rate. This analysis shows that for 2012, bike share usage was responsible for 115,826 km less car driving in Melbourne, through to 632,841 km in London. Washington, D.C., despite having almost ten times greater bike share travel than Brisbane, only has approximately 3.5 times the car use reduction impact. This difference is due to a *car substitution* rate of 21% for Brisbane, compared to only 7% for Washington, D.C. (see Figure 4.1).

Figure 4.2 extends the analysis to also include the truck travel performed by the bike share operator to rebalance bikes. The results show that for each kilometre travelled by motorised vehicles associated with the operation of bike share programs, there are between 2 and 4 km of private car use avoided, with the exception of London, in which the relationship is reversed.

The results indicate an estimated reduction in motor vehicle use due to bike share of approximately 90,000 km per annum in Melbourne and Minneapolis/St. Paul and 243,291 km for Washington, D.C. London's bike share program, however, recorded an *additional* 766,341 km in motor vehicle use. London, owing to its car mode substitution rate of only 2% (see Figure 4.1), coupled with heavy demand for fleet redistribution, is estimated to have approximately 2.2 km in motor vehicle support travel for each kilometre of private car use avoided. To illustrate the influence of mode substitution, should the percentage of bike share trips substituting for car increase to 10% in London, estimated car travel reduction would rise to 3.1 million km, approximately 2.2 times greater than the distance travelled by motor vehicle support services (Fishman, Washington, & Haworth, 2014).

The results of this analysis demonstrate that in order for bike share programs to optimise their impact on reducing car use, it is necessary to implement measures focused on encouraging those currently making trips by car to use bike share. Results from a survey of non–bike share users from Brisbane (see Fishman, Washington, Haworth, & Mazzei, 2014) suggest that this may be best achieved via policy changes that seek to increase the *competitive advantage* of bike share over the convenience of car use, and

Table 4.1 Bike share size, usage and car travel reduction

	Melbourne	Brisbane	Washington, D.C.	Minnesota	London[a]
Bikes[b]	600	1,800	1,800	1,325	8,000
Trips[c] (2012)	138,548	209,232	2,008,079	268,151	9,040,580
Trips per day per bike	0.6	0.3	3.0	0.9	3.1
Regional population[d]	3,999,980	2,065,998	5,860,342	3,759,978	7,170,000
Mean trip duration[c]	22.0	16.2	15.8	17.5	17.5
Est. travel speed (km/h)	12	12	12	12	12
Est. distance travelled per trip (km)	4.4	3.2	3.1	3.5	3.5
Est. distance travelled per system 2012 (km)	609,611	677,912	6,345,530	940,152	31,642,029
Car substitution	19%	21%	7%	19%	2%
Est. car travel reduction (km)	115,826	142,361	444,187	182,390	632,841
Est. car travel reduction per bike (km)	193	79	247	135	79
Annual members	921	1,926	18,000	3,500	76,283

Source: Regional population: Brisbane and Melbourne (Australian Bureau of Statistics, 2013), London (Greater London Authority, 2012), Minnesota (Minneapolis/St. Paul Combined Statistical Area) (Wikipedia, 2013) and Washington, Metropolitan Area (Wikipedia, 2012). Trips and duration: Melbourne (Hoernel, Unpublished data), Brisbane (Lundberg, Unpublished data), Minnesota (Vars, Unpublished data), London (Stanhope, Unpublished data), Washington, D.C. (Capital Bikeshare, 2013), Estimated travel speed (Jensen, Rouquier, Ovtracht, & Robardet, 2010). Car substitution (Fishman, Washington, & Haworth, 2013).

a In March 2012, London's bike share fleet rose from approximately 6,000 bikes to 8,000 bikes. Serco (bike share operator) experienced data loss between 1 January–3 January and 5 February–28 February 2012. Estimates used for missing trip data during these dates based on activity either side of data loss period. Trips less than 4 minutes duration are removed by Serco between 29 April and 18 August 2012 (unrecoverable).

b Fleet total, which may not reflect actual number of bicycles in circulation.

c Trips <2 minutes and >3 hours excluded from analysis.

d Method of demarcating regional boundaries differs and those interested are encouraged to examine cited sources.

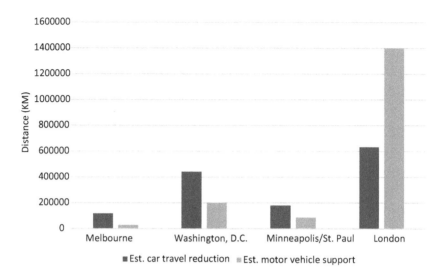

Figure 4.2 Comparing car use reduction with motor vehicle support, selected
  cities, 2012.
Source: Fishman, Washington and Haworth (2014).

improving perceptions of rider safety, through the development of a network of protected bicycle lanes and paths.

Whilst truck movements from bike share operators to undertake rebalancing are identified as harming the positive influence bike share can
have on cities (Médard de Chardon et al., 2017), there are some encouraging early results from programs designed to minimise the need for trucks
to undertake rebalancing. As described in Chapter 8, some bike share
operators have successfully introduced programs that encourage members the members themselves to undertake rebalancing tasks. Members
typically rebalance bicycles either by riding the bike to an empty/under-
supplied station or walking two bikes at a time. These programs should
be encouraged as they can be a cost- and emission-effective method of
keeping bike share systems in balance.

As noted in the introduction, a growing number of cities have a policy ambition to reduce car use, especially for short to medium journeys.
The planning of a new bike share program should therefore attempt to
create a system that maximises the likelihood of reducing car use to the
greatest extent possible. Designing a system to increase use by those who
would have otherwise taken a short car trip should be an over-riding
principle. For this to occur, marketing efforts attracting car drivers may
be necessary. Marketing is just one method of doing this, and these activities will be more effective if the system increases the *value proposition* of

bike share relative to car use. An example of such an approach would be a complementary policy of an increase in the cost and decrease in supply of inner city car parking. Whilst recognising the potential divisiveness of this issue, it is clear that the most successful bike share cities are all in places where car use is expensive and difficult (Fishman, 2015). These changes (i.e., enhanced convenience and safety of cycling relative to short car trips) will of course not just enhance bike share's performance but will also enhance overall sustainable mobility choice in cities (Pucher & Buehler, 2017).

4.2 Improved Transport Choice

Enhanced mobility options and convenience are two of the strongest, most consistent themes to emerge from research on why people use bike share (Fishman, 2015; Shaheen, Cohen, & Martin, 2013). Bike share has proven popular to combine with public transport, helping to make up for the inevitable deficiencies in the coverage or frequency of a city's public transport system (Fishman, Washington, Haworth, et al., 2014). Bike share presents a relatively affordable method of providing greater levels of accessibility to the public transport network (see Section 11.3). Providing cycle networks that connect communities that are outside a short walk to train stations can increase the catchment of public transport by a factor of 15 (Hudson, 1982).

Another element of enhanced transport choice associated with bike share is improved *transport flexibility.* Unlike private cycling, bike share offers the user with the freedom to easily make *one-way* cycling trips, and select another mode for a component of their day's travel, should it offer greater convenience. For instance, if it were raining in the morning, one might use public transport and then opt for bike share if conditions became more favourable in the afternoon. Bike share enables people to cycle the component of the journey that makes sense to cycle, leaving other transport options available when it does not (unencumbered by a private bike). A number of studies have also found that around 5%–8% of trips taken on bike share are *new* journeys, which would not have taken place had it not been for the availability of the bike share system (Fishman, 2015). A similar percentage of bike share trips replace *private bike* trips.

In addition to helping to integrate cycling with public transport and provide increased transport flexibility, one of the most important motivations for bike share users comes from *increased travel time competitiveness.* For journeys that would involve multiple transfers on public transport, lengthy walks and outside of peak travel (reduced frequency of service), bike share may represent a faster option, for short to medium trip lengths.

The same is true for car trips that involve heavy congestion or parking difficulties.

One of the most important themes within this book is that people do not make transport mode decisions in isolation. The decision to use bike share will usually be as a result of weighing up the pros and cons of the different modes available. When bike share feels safe, is relatively fast and low cost, there is a heightened possibility it will be favoured over other modes. It is critical, therefore, that planners of bike share programs adopt a 'thinking like a rider' mentality when designing a bike share system. This helps create a system that offers a more compelling value proposition to potential users. As the benefits of bike share are always dependent on the degree to which it is used, it must be designed to be competitive with other modes of transport, especially short car trips, if it is to maximise the benefits it offers.

Bike share has also been shown to increase the resilience and adaptability of the transport system. Studies have shown that when public transport fails (e.g., through a strike), bike share usage *increases*. For instance, Saberi, Ghamami, Gu, Shojaei and Fishman (2018) studied the impact of the London tube strike of 2015, via an analysis of over 1 million bike share trips. They found that during the period of the strike, the number of trips on London's bike share system increased and the average duration also increased dramatically, from 23 to 43 minutes. The researchers concluded that bike share can act to increase the resilience of transport networks, by providing a more flexible solution that can help to make up for the deficiency caused by public transport disruptions.

Bike share should not, however, be seen as mealy a competitor or replacement of public transport journeys. A consistent theme emerging from research is that bike share users regularly integrate their rides with public transport. For instance, an evaluation of dockless bike share usage in Seattle found that 75% of respondents had used bike share to access public transport and a third regularly access public transport with bike share (Seattle Department of Transportation, 2017).

4.3 Population Health

Sedentary lifestyles represent one of the most significant threats to population health and life expectancy (Garrard, 2009; World Health Organisation, 2010). Over half the population in many countries do not undertake sufficient levels of physical activity to protect against sedentary lifestyle diseases such as diabetes, hypertension and heart disease (Bauman et al., 2009). In fact, it is estimated that physical inactivity causes 21%–25% of the burden of disease from breast and colon cancer and even greater proportions for diabetes (27%) and ischaemic heart disease (30%) (World Health Organisation, 2009). The World Health Organisation recommends that healthy adults (18–64 years old) should engage in a minimum of 150 minutes of moderate intensity aerobic activity throughout the week (World Health Organisation, 2010), and bike use has been found to achieve the necessary intensity to qualify for moderate-intensity activity (Ainsworth et al., 2011; Gojanovic, Welker, Iglesias, Daucourt, & Gremion, 2011; Simons, Van Es, & Hendriksen, 2009).

The problem of sedentary lifestyle disease (inactivity) and cycling's ability to increase physical activity is well established (Götschi, Garrard, & Giles-Corti, 2015). The positive impact cycling can have on overall population health has been part of the reasons cities invest in bike share. One of the great, long-standing challenges for city planners is how to 're-engineer' physical activity back into the lifestyles of urban populations (Dora & Phillips, 2000). These populations have become increasingly employed in sedentary occupations within service or knowledge industries (this author included!). The introduction of a bike share program within a city is one measure governments can take to help reverse the trend caused by the 'obesogenic' environments many cities have become.

Sedentary lifestyle disease is not the only population health issue bike share can influence. Air quality, transport safety and mental health are additional issues in which bike share has shown some impact in addressing. Several studies have attempted to quantify the health impacts of bike share, with some focused on one outcome variable, such as changes to physical activity levels, whilst others attempt to capture a larger range of outcomes. The most comprehensive examination of the health impacts of bike share was published in the *British Medical Journal* by Woodcock, Tainio, Cheshire, O'Brien and Goodman (2014) and focused on the London bike share program. The researchers focused on three issues: *physical activity*, *crashes* and *exposure to air pollution*. This study used trip data to model the health impacts of the program via comparison to a scenario in which the program did not exist. Physical activity was found to increase considerably at the population level. The associated benefits were shown to differ by gender and age, with men's major benefit coming from reductions in ischaemic heart disease, whereas women were more likely to benefit in terms of reductions in depression.

In relation to crashes, the results of the Woodcock et al. (2014) study suggest that on balance, the program delivers more benefit than harm, although the effects are not uniform for all age groups or genders. Interestingly, the researchers found that more benefit would be gained if users were older, as older people have fewer healthy life years to lose (if involved in a crash). When the researchers applied the general crash risk for all cycling in central London, they found a negative health impact for women, due to the greater fatality rate among female cyclists in London (Woodcock et al., 2014). However, since the data were collected, Transport for London have made major upgrades to their cycling network (Transport for London, 2017), and this is likely to reduce the crash risk and thus further tip the balance of safety benefits in favour of bike share's existence. Further analysis of bike share's impact on safety can be found in Section 4.4. In terms of air pollution, the study found little impact on air pollution exposure to the riders themselves (Woodcock et al., 2014).

In the first multi-city analysis of the physical activity impacts of bike share, Fishman, Washington and Haworth (2015) attempted to develop an estimate of the changes in physical activity levels due to bike share. Using data collected from the bike share systems in Melbourne, Brisbane, Washington, D.C., London and Minneapolis/St. Paul, the researchers were interested in the *net changes* in physical activity by examining transfers from sedentary to active modes. The researchers used the mode substitution rates shown earlier in Figure 4.1. Given that a kilometre walked consumes more energy than a kilometre cycled (Fishman, Böcker, & Helbich, 2015), the researchers needed to account for bike share trips that were previously walked, as this resulted in a *net loss* of physical activity.

In order to sufficiently account for shifts between walking and bike share an assumption was made that a bike share trip substituting for walking would be one-third the duration of the same trip done on foot. The basis of this assumption is that typical walking speed is approximately one-third the average bike share speed. For example, a 15-minute walk would translate to about a 5-minute bike share journey.

Related to the above assumption, a second assumption was that when a person substitutes walking for bike share, the average bike share journey will only be five minutes in duration. This assumption is based on the fact that when bike share substitutes for walking, the trip by foot is highly likely to have been substantially shorter than a trip that, for example, substitutes for a car or public transport journey. For instance, a typical bike share journey is around 16 minutes (Fishman, Washington, & Haworth, 2014). If such a bike share trip had taken place on foot instead, the journey would have taken approximately 45–50 minutes, which is considerably longer than most urban walking trips (Central Bureau of Statistics, 2014; Merom, van der Ploeg, Corpuz, & Bauman, 2010; Transport for London, 2011b). In London, the average walking trip is about 17 minutes (Transport for London, 2011b). Finally, when an individual transfers from walking to bike share, they save time (as cycling is faster than walking). In this analysis, it is assumed the saved time was not used to engage in moderate or intense physical activity.

The results suggest an average of 60% of bike share trips replace sedentary modes, but when bike share replaces walking, a net *reduction* in physical activity results. Overall, however, bike share was found to have a positive impact on physical activity (see Figure 4.3), leading to an additional 74 million minutes of physical activity in London through to 1.4 million minutes of physical activity in Minneapolis/St. Paul, for 2012.

A Markov Chain Monte Carlo (MCMC) simulation was used to estimate the minutes of additional active travel due to bike share, as shown in Table 4.2. In essence what Table 4.2 provides is the sum of the positive impact of bike share on active travel, minus the negative effect when bike share replaces a trip previously made by foot. Figures are in 'million minutes'.

The correct interpretation of the confidence intervals shown in Table 4.2 is that if a system was set up just like Brisbane, 95 out of 100 systems would yield an increase in active travel of between 1.72 and 2.02 million minutes per year as a result of switches from other modes to bike share trips. The uncertainty estimates account for the uncertainty in reported trip durations, mode shares and reported total number of trips by system operators. The London system had the largest impact on active travel, with between 68.9 and 80.8 million additional minutes of active travel per year with 95% confidence.

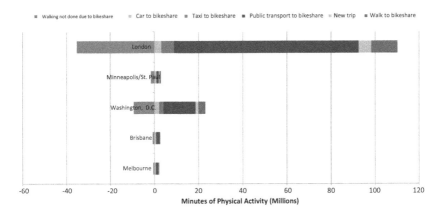

Figure 4.3 Estimated changes to active travel due to bike share.
Source: Fishman, Washington and Haworth (2015).

Table 4.2 Estimated millions of minutes of additional active travel due to bike share

City	2.5% CI	5% CI	Median	95% CI	97.5% CI
Brisbane	1.72	1.73	1.86	2.00	2.02
Melbourne	1.38	1.40	1.55	1.73	1.79
Minneapolis/St. Paul	1.24	1.24	1.40	1.60	1.65
Washington, D.C.	12.11	12.35	13.80	15.55	16.10
London	67.91	68.90	74.37	80.80	82.23

Source: Fishman, Washington, and Haworth (2015).
NB: CI is Confidence Interval.

Some caution needs to be exercised when interpreting the results reported in this research by Fishman, Washington and Haworth (2014). The underlying physical activity level of bike share users is not known and therefore has not been incorporated into the analysis. One needs to be mindful of this when attributing physical activity benefits to bike share use, as the benefits associated with physical activity are *dose dependent* (Foulds, Bredin, Charlesworth, Ivey, & Warburton, 2014). If an individual's level of physical activity already meets guidelines, additional physical activity through bike share may provide little health benefit, whilst continuing to expose the user to injury risk. It is also possible that bike share users are forgoing other forms of physical activity (such as going to the gym), due to their bike share usage.

4.4 Bike Share and Safety

Prior to the introduction of bike share in cities such as New York, some analysts had forecast a rise in the number of bicycle crashes. Empirical research on bike share safety is in its infancy. This section will examine the impact bike share programs have on cycling safety. Bike share safety has attracted a lot of attention within the mainstream media (Bernstein, 2014). Prior to the introduction of North America's largest bike share program in New York City, a bicycle researcher was quoted in the New York Times predicting 'at least a doubling and possibly even a tripling in injuries and fatalities among cyclists and pedestrians during the first year' (Flegenheimer, 2013). Thankfully, these predictions have failed to materialise, and there is now an active sub-sector of the transport safety community examining why bike share appears to have a better safety record to cycling on private bikes.

Over a decade ago, Jacobsen (2003) published a landmark paper describing what has become known as 'Safety in Numbers', showing that cyclists are less likely to be injured when volumes of cyclists are higher. As of December 2017, only two fatalities have been recorded among those using US bike share programs (Chicago and New York City). The fatality on Citi Bike occurred after 43 million trips had taken place since the system launched in May 2013. Whilst the incidence of serious and fatal injuries appears to be lower than some initially expected, it is important to remember that may governments have adopted a *Vision Zero* approach to road safety, where the acceptable level of traffic fatality is *zero*. This means there is always more than can be done to reduce death and serious injury, and this includes when designing bike share programs and the streets and paths at enable their use.

This section attempts to provide an overview of what is currently known about bike share and safety and concludes by offering some recommendations to take a more systematic approach to the recording of crashes that occur on bike share.

4.4.1 What the Data Say about Bike Share Safety?

Bike share safety research straddles the sustainable transport and population health/safety fields. A somewhat volatile debate was sparked by an article published in the *American Journal of Public Health* (see Graves et al., 2014) that assessed hospital injury data from five US cities with bike share programs and five without. The analysis occurred during a 24-month period *before* bike share implementation and also for a 12-month period *post* implementation. The non–bike share cities essentially acted as a control. What the researchers found, but failed to include in their discussion, was the dramatic *reduction* in the total number of hospital-recorded injuries in the bike share cities, post implementation. Figure 4.4 uses data collected by Graves et al. (2014) to illustrate the reduction in recorded injuries in bike share cities compared to a slight *increase* in control cities (no bike share).

The conclusions by Graves et al. (2014), which have been criticised by other scholars (e.g., see Teschke & Winters, 2014; Woodcock & Goodman, 2014), were for bike share operators to provide helmets, despite a clear *reduction* in the number of head injuries for bike share cities. The data reported by Graves et al. (2014) are especially significant when considering that the overall amount of cycling *increases* after the introduction of a bike share program. This is consistent with the *Safety in Numbers* phenomenon (e.g., see Elvik, 2009), in which a rise in the amount of cycling does not lead to a proportional rise in the number of injuries.

Figure 4.5 provides an overview of the type of crashes recorded on the Montreal bike share program, indicating that of the crashes reported, almost half involved a motor vehicle. Few bike share operators provide data

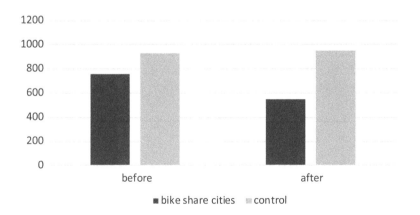

Figure 4.4 Injuries (all types), bike share cities and non–bike share cities (control). Source: Graves et al. (2014).

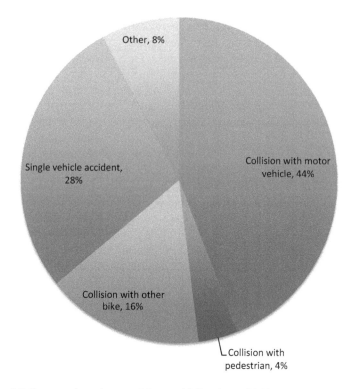

Figure 4.5 Reported crash type, Montreal bike share, 2013.
Source: BIXI Montreal (*BIXI Accident Data 2013*, 2014, Personal Communication).

on the type of crashes reported on their system and as will be described below, there is a lack of consistency with which bike share operators record crash data.

Research from North America reveals bike share to be perceived as safer, and objectively safer than private bike riding (Martin, Cohen, Botha, & Shaheen, 2016). The fact that bike share bikes are usually bigger, slower and more robust than private bikes is key to their better safety record. Some researchers have also found bike share riders perceive that drivers become more considerate when passing bike share riders compared to riders of private bikes (Fishman, Washington, & Haworth, 2012; Martin et al., 2016).

In the first multi-country assessment of bike share safety that includes exposure factors, Fishman and Schepers (2016) assessed both the distance travelled and the number of reported injuries on bike share for 2013 in various US, European and Australian cities. Table 4.3 illustrates the number of reported injuries, which have been categorised as either *slight* injury, *serious* injury or *fatality*.

Figure 4.6 compares the injury rates of the Paris and London bike share programs to the injury rates in the jurisdictions of which these are part. For both levels of severity and both bike share programs, the injury rates are lower for bike share. This is consistent with the estimates for fatality rates and may show actual safety differences. Readers interested in examining the methodology used to derive the data presented in Figure 4.6 are encouraged to see the full paper, published in the *Journal of Safety Research* (see Fishman & Schepers, 2016).

The results presented in Figure 4.6 suggest that bike share users are less likely than other cyclists to sustain fatal, severe or slight injuries. A relatively reliable measure for this is the fatality rate which was in the same range as the safest cycling countries in the world, the Netherlands and Denmark. According to the results of this analysis, a bike share user is

Table 4.3 Reported incidents to bike share operators, selected cities, 2013

	Slight injury	*Serious injury*	*Fatal*
Paris	159	19	0
London	62	17	1
New York City	71	9	0
Montreal	22	0	0
Washington, D.C.	23	2	0
Chicago	5	2	0
Minneapolis/St. Paul	0	0	0
Melbourne	0	0	0
All city total	342	49	1

Source: Fishman and Schepers (2016).

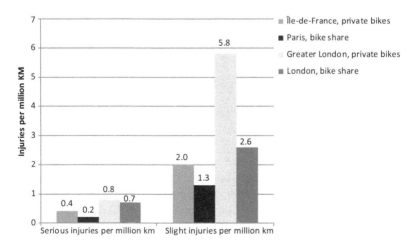

Figure 4.6 Injuries per million kilometre travelled.
Source: Fishman and Schepers (2016).

half as likely to be fatally injured, per kilometre travelled, than a general cyclist, in jurisdictions in which a bike share program operates. However, the number of fatalities on which this comparison is based is still relatively low. Comparing serious and slight injuries leads to the same conclusion, but this comparison is hampered by the fact that the bike share data were based on information reported to operators whilst the numbers for other cyclists were based on police-reported crashes. Although there are uncertainties, the fact that the literature and outcomes for all levels of injury severity point in the same direction yields some support for lower risk for bike share users compared to other cyclists.

One explanation for the higher levels of safety for bike share use might be that their speeds are substantially lower than for other cyclists. Bike share speeds are generally in the same range as the Netherlands. A slower speed increases the time available for cyclists to react to avoid crashes that may have occurred at higher velocities. It is also possible that motorists perceive bike share users to be less experienced and/or tourists and therefore display a greater level of caution, as revealed in qualitative research on perceptions of bike share (Fishman et al., 2012). The notion that drivers behave differently depending on the appearance of the cyclist has been established by Walker (2007) who found that drivers overtook closer to helmeted cyclists compared to those without a helmet. The upright position of bike share bikes may improve cyclists' visual observation of the road environment, potentially helping to avoid crashes. Finally, most bike share systems occupy the inner area of cities, which typically have better bicycle infrastructure than outer suburbs. Protected bike infrastructure is known to reduce crash risk between cyclists and motor vehicle drivers (Teschke et al., 2012).

4.4.2 Summary and Implications

The overall theme from this review of the literature examining bike share and health is that bike share has positive population health implications. Bike share's impact on physical activity is positive, and as such, is helpful in addressing the diseases caused by a sedentary lifestyle (e.g., diabetes, heart disease, depression). Importantly, the health benefits of bike share outweigh the health risks riders are exposed to in terms of road traffic injury and air pollution.

One of the most startling findings is that bike share users appear to be less exposed to crash risk than private cyclists. This is consistent with the aforementioned *safety in numbers* phenomenon and suggests that cities that introduce bike share may be offering a protective mechanism to reduce the risk of riding. Whilst this most obviously applies to those on bike share bikes, there may also be some risk reduction effect to private cyclists as well, if bike share helps to make drivers more aware of the possibility of encountering cyclists (reducing the so-called 'looked but did not see phenomenon'). Moreover, if bike share is introduced with a host of other supportive measures, particularly protected bicycle infrastructure and other initiatives to improve a city's bicycle friendliness (as was the case in cities like Paris and New York),[4] it is more than plausible that the safety of all people choosing to cycle (bike share and private) will be enhanced.

Finally, this review has found that current bike share operators have not yet established a consistent reporting methodology for capturing crashes. The development and implementation of a standardised, industry-wide reporting tool needs to be developed and built into the contract cities develop when establishing or renewing bike share agreements with providers/operators. The dockless bike share industry, owing to its ability to launch bike share without public subsidy, does not yet have any consistent, industry-wide method for collecting crash data. This is something that city governments will need to encourage/enforce, as without such a measure, it will not be possible to measure the level of risk/safety riders are exposed to. As technologies continue to be integrated onto the bikes that make up modern bike share fleets, there is a growing opportunity to use these sensors and tracking technologies to build up a more detailed picture of crashes, where and when they occur, the speed of the rider, etc. Using accelerometers, it may be possible for operators to predict when a crash may have occurred and send a push notification through the App to ask the rider whether such an incident has taken place. A universal crash data collection tool is needed. The following attributes should be included:

- Name
- Date of birth
- Gender
- Crash date
- Crash time
- Crash location (using online mapping tool to provide geo-coordinates)
- Crash type
- Have police attended
- Injury severity
- Injury details
- Customer consent for safety researchers to contact victim
- Contact details.

For most of the above categories, drop-down boxes with short explanations to guide the operator should be used, in order to maintain consistency in reporting.

In addition to the above benefits of bike share, it has also been found that bike share helps to normalise the image of cycling (Goodman, Green, & Woodcock, 2013). This is important in cities with very low bike mode share (less than ~4% of trips) because it is very often the case that cycling is seen by many to be a marginalised activity that is restricted to so-called 'MAMILS' (middle-aged men in Lycra). Goodman et al. (2013) found that bike share riders in London were more likely to ride wearing regular clothes, with a gender balance closer to the population average. Bike share may therefore act to normalise cycling as an everyday transport option, rather than a sporting activity only available to a narrow segment of the population.

Finally, as bike share programs continue to grow, it is important for industry standards to become established that make evaluation easier, more transparent and enable comparison between different programs.

Notes

1 Unlike private bicycle use, bike share more easily allows the rider to ride one leg of a journey without the impost of cycling the return journey, say for instance if the weather turns unfavourable.
2 The overall impact of bike share on public transport is not yet clear and is unlikely to have a uniform direction. As discussed in Chapter 11, some researchers have found bike share can act to *increase* overall public transport ridership (e.g. see Ma, Liu, & Erdoğan, 2015).
3 See Fishman, Washington and Haworth (2014) for a quantitative assessment comparing bike share's impact on car use with truck trips generated due to rebalancing of bikes.
4 The absence of a concerted effort to substantially enhance the network of protected bicycle lanes/paths in Melbourne and Brisbane has been noted as one of the contributing factors to the low usage levels that have characterised these programs. A bike share program in a city with a street network that does not meet the safety expectations of its intended market runs the risk of underuse.

References

Ainsworth, B. E., Haskell, W. L., Herrmann, S. D., Meckes, N., Bassett, D. R., Jr., Tudor-Locke, C., … Leon, A. S. (2011). 2011 Compendium of physical activities: A second update of codes and MET values. *Medicine & Science in Sports & Exercise, 43*(8), 1575–1581. doi:10.1249/MSS.0b013e31821ece12

Australian Bureau of Statistics. (2013). Census 2011. Retrieved from http://www.abs.gov.au/websitedbs/censushome.nsf/home/data?opendocument&navpos=200

Bauman, A., Bull, F., Chey, T., Craig, C. L., Ainsworth, B. E., Sallis, J. F., … Pratt, M. (2009). The international prevalence study on physical activity: Results from 20 countries. *International Journal of Behavioral Nutrition and Physical Activity, 6*, 21. doi:10.1186/1479-5868-6-21

Bernstein, L. (2014). Proportion of Head Injuries Rises in Cities with Bike Share Programs. *Washington Post.* Retrieved from http://www.washingtonpost.com/news/to-your-health/wp/2014/06/12/cities-with-bike-share-programs-see-rise-in-cyclist-head-injuries/

Capital Bikeshare. (2013). Trip History Data. Retrieved from https://www.capitalbikeshare.com/trip-history-data

Central Bureau of Statistics. (2014). *Research Travel in Netherlands (OViN)*. The Netherlands: Central Bureau of Statistics. Retrieved from http://www. cbs.nl/nl-NL/menu/themas/verkeer-vervoer/methoden/dataverzameling/ korte-onderzoeksbeschrijvingen/ovin-beschrijving-art.htm

Dora, C., & Phillips, M. A. (2000). Transport, Environment, and Health (9289013567, 9789289013567). Retrieved from Copenhagen: http://libcat. library.qut.edu.au/record=b2999557&searchscope=8

Elvik, R. (2009). The non-linearity of risk and the promotion of environmentally sustainable transport. *Accident Analysis & Prevention, 41*(4), 849–855.

Fishman, E. (2014). *Bikeshare: Barriers, facilitators and impacts on car use* (PhD thesis by publication). Queensland University of Technology, Brisbane.

Fishman, E. (2015). Bikeshare: A review of recent literature. *Transport Reviews*, 1–22. doi:10.1080/01441647.2015.1033036

Fishman, E., Böcker, L., & Helbich, M. (2015). Adult active transport in the Netherlands: An analysis of its contribution to physical activity requirements. *PloS ONE, 10*(4), e0121871. doi:10.1371/journal.pone.0121871

Fishman, E., & Schepers, J. P. (2016). Global bike share: What the data tells us about road safety. *Journal of Safety Research, 56*, 41–45.

Fishman, E., Washington, S., & Haworth, N. (2012). Barriers and facilitators to public bicycle scheme use: A qualitative approach. *Transportation Research Part F-Traffic Psychology and Behaviour, 15*(6), 686–698.

Fishman, E., Washington, S., & Haworth, N. (2013). Bike share: A synthesis of the literature. *Transport Reviews, 33*(2), 148–165. doi:10.1080/01441647.2013.775612

Fishman, E., Washington, S., & Haworth, N. (2014). Bike share's impact on car use: Evidence from the United States, Great Britain, and Australia. *Transportation Research Part D: Transport & Environment, 31*, 7. doi:10.1016/j.trd.2014.05.013

Fishman, E., Washington, S., & Haworth, N. (2015). Bikeshare's impact on active travel: Evidence from the United States, Great Britain, and Australia. *Journal of Transport & Health, 2*(2), 135–142. doi:10.1016/j.jth.2015.03.004

Fishman, E., Washington, S., Haworth, N., & Mazzei, A. (2014). Barriers to bikesharing: An analysis from Melbourne and Brisbane. *Journal of Transport Geography, 41*, 325–337.

Flegenheimer, M. (2013). No Riders Killed in First 5 Months of New York City Bike-Share Program. *New York Times*. Retrieved from http://www.nytimes. com/2013/11/05/nyregion/no-riders-killed-in-first-5-months-of-new-york-city-bike-share-program.html?_r=0

Foulds, H. J. A., Bredin, S. S. D., Charlesworth, S. A., Ivey, A. C., & Warburton, D. E. R. (2014). Exercise volume and intensity: A dose-response relationship with health benefits. *European Journal of Applied Physiology, 114*, 1563–1571.

Garrard, J. (2009). Taking Action on Obesogenic Environments: Building a Culture of Active, Connected Communities. Retrieved from http://www.health. gov.au/internet/preventativehealth/publishing.nsf/Content/0FBE203C-1C547A82CA257529000231BF/$File/commpaper-obes-env-garrard.pdf

Gojanovic, B., Welker, J., Iglesias, K., Daucourt, C., & Gremion, G. (2011). Electric bicycles as a new active transportation modality to promote health. *Medicine & Science in Sports & Exercise, 43*(11), 2204–2210.

Goodman, A., Green, J., & Woodcock, J. (2013). The role of bicycle sharing systems in normalising the image of cycling: An observational study of London cyclists. *Journal of Transport & Health, 1*(1), 5–8. doi:10.1016/j.jth.2013.07.001

Götschi, T., Garrard, J., & Giles-Corti, B. (2015). Cycling as a part of daily life: A review of health perspectives. *Transport Reviews*, 1–27. doi:10.1080/0144164 7.2015.1057877

Graves, J. M., Pless, B., Moore, L., Nathens, A. B., Hunte, G., & Rivara, F. P. (2014). Public bicycle share programs and head injuries. *American Journal of Public Health*, e1–e6. doi:10.2105/AJPH.2014.302012

Greater London Authority. (2012). *Census 2011 London Boroughs' Population by Age and Sex*. London: Greater London Authority. Retrieved from http://data. london.gov.uk/datastorefiles/documents/2011-census-first-results.pdf

Hudson, M. (1982). *Bicycle Planning: Policy and Practice*. London: Architectural Press.

Jacobsen, P. L. (2003). Safety in numbers: More walkers and bicyclists, safer walking and bicycling. *Injury Prevention, 9*(3), 205–209.

Jensen, P., Rouquier, J.-B., Ovtracht, N., & Robardet, C. (2010). Characterizing the speed and paths of shared bicycle use in Lyon. *Transportation Research Part D, 15*(8), 522–524. doi:10.1016/j.trd.2010.07.002

LDA Consulting. (2012). Capital Bikeshare 2011 Member Survey Report. Retrieved from Washington, DC.: https://d21xlh2maitm24.cloudfront.net/wdc/ Capital-Bikeshare-SurveyReport-Final.pdf?mtime=20161206135935

LDA Consulting. (2013). 2013 Capital Bikeshare Member Survey Report. Retrieved from Washington, DC: http://capitalbikeshare.com/assets/pdf/CABI-2013SurveyReport.pdf

LDA Consulting. (2017). 2016 Capital Bikeshare Member Survey Report. Retrieved from Washington, DC: https://d21xlh2maitm24.cloudfront.net/wdc/ Capital-Bikeshare_2016MemberSurvey_Executive-Summary.pdf?mtime= 20170303165533

Ma, T., Liu, C., & Erdoğan, S. (2015). Bicycle sharing and public transit: Does capital bikeshare affect metrorail ridership in Washington, DC? In *Vol. 2534*. *Transportation Research Record* (pp. 1–9). National Research Council: https:// trid.trb.org/view/1339357

Martin, E., Cohen, A., Botha, J., & Shaheen, S. (2016). *Bikesharing and Bicycle Safety*. Retrieved from San Jose: http://transweb.sjsu.edu/PDFs/research/1204-bikesharing-and-bicycle-safety.pdf

Médard de Chardon, C., Caruso, G., & Thomas, I. (2017). Bicycle sharing system 'success' determinants. *Transportation Research Part A: Policy and Practice, 100*, 202–214.

Merom, D., van der Ploeg, H. P., Corpuz, G., & Bauman, A. E. (2010). Public health perspectives on household travel surveys: Active travel between 1997 and 2007. *American Journal of Preventive Medicine, 39*(2), 113–121.

Nice Ride Minnesota. (2010). Nice Ride Minnesota Survey November 2010. Retrieved from http://appv3.sgizmo.com/reportsview/?key=102593-416326-6d13ea0276ea0822c9f59f4411b6c779

Pucher, J., & Buehler, R. (2017). Trends in walking and cycling safety in high-income countries, with a focus on the United States and Germany. *American Journal of Public Health, 107*, 281–287.

Saberi, M., Ghamami, M., Gu, Y., Shojaei, M. H., & Fishman, E. (2018). Understanding the impacts of a public transit disruption on bicycle sharing mobility patterns: A case of tube strike in London. *Journal of Transport Geography, 66*, 154–166. doi:10.1016/j.jtrangeo.2017.11.018

Seattle Department of Transportation. (2017). 2017 Free-floating Bike Share Pilot Evaluation Report. Retrieved from Seattle: https://www.seattle.gov/Documents/Departments/SDOT/BikeProgram/2017BikeShareEvaluationReport.pdf

Shaheen, S., Cohen, A. P., & Martin, E. W. (2013). Public bikesharing in North America: Early operator understanding and emerging trends. *Transportation Research Record: Journal of the Transportation Research Board, 2387*, 83–92. doi:10.3141/2387-10

Simons, M., Van Es, E., & Hendriksen, I. (2009). Electrically assisted cycling: A new mode for meeting physical activity guidelines? *Medicine and Science in Sports and Exercise, 41*(11), 2097–2102.

Teschke, K., Harris, M. A., Reynolds, C. C. O., Winters, M., Babul, S., Chipman, M., … Cripton, P. A. (2012). Route infrastructure and the risk of injuries to bicyclists: A case-crossover study. *American Journal of Public Health, 102*(12), 2336–2343. doi:10.2105/AJPH.2012.300762

Teschke, K., & Winters, M. (2014). Letter to editor. *American Journal of Public Health*. Retrieved from http://cyclingincities-spph.sites.olt.ubc.ca/files/2014/06/Graves-AJPH-as-submitted.pdf

Transport for London. (2011a). *Barclays Cycle Hire Customer Satisfaction and Usage – Wave 2*. London: Transport for London.

Transport for London. (2011b). *Travel in London Report 4*. London: Transport for London. Retrieved from http://www.tfl.gov.uk/cdn/static/cms/documents/travel-in-london-report-4.pdf

Transport for London. (2017). *Draft Mayor's Transport Strategy*. London: Transport for London. Retrieved from https://tfl.gov.uk/corporate/about-tfl/how-we-work/planning-for-the-future/the-mayors-transport-strategy

Walker, I. (2007). Drivers overtaking bicyclists: Objective data on the effects of riding position, helmet use, vehicle type and apparent gender. *Accident Analysis & Prevention, 39*(2), 417–425. doi:10.1016/j.aap.2006.08.010

Wikipedia. (2012). Washington Metropolitan Area. Retrieved from http://en.wikipedia.org/wiki/Washington-Arlington-Alexandria,_DC-VA-MD-WV_Metropolitan_Statistical_Area#Metropolitan_Statistical_Area

Wikipedia. (2013). Minneapolis-Saint Paul. Retrieved from http://en.wikipedia.org/wiki/Minneapolis%E2%80%93Saint_Paul

Woodcock, J., & Goodman, A. (2014). Hard Evidence: Do Bikeshare Schemes Lead to More Head Injuries among Cyclists? Retrieved from http://theconversation.com/hard-evidence-do-bikeshare-schemes-lead-to-more-head-injuries-among-cyclists-30135

Woodcock, J., Tainio, M., Cheshire, J., O'Brien, O., & Goodman, A. (2014). Health effects of the London bicycle sharing system: Health impact modelling study. *BMJ, 348*. doi:10.1136/bmj.g425

World Health Organisation. (2009). Global Health Risks: Mortality and Burden of Disease Attributable to Selected Major Risks. Retrieved from Geneva: http://www.who.int/healthinfo/global_burden_disease/GlobalHealthRisks_report_full.pdf?ua=1

World Health Organisation. (2010). Global Recommendations on Physical Activity for Health. Retrieved from Geneva: http://whqlibdoc.who.int/publications/2010/9789241599979_eng.pdf

5 Demographics of Bike Share Users

The demographics of bike share users has become a common focus of attention for bike share operators, researchers and the media. The media's interest in the demographics of bike share users has been sparked by a relatively consistent finding that people those use bike share, at least in the United Kingdom and North America, tend to be wealthier, Caucasian and better educated than the general population. Even within the first year of the London bike share program, it had attracted attention for skewed demographic it seemed to attract (Lewis, 2011).

The media's interest in bike share tendency to attract more privileged members of society is often underpinned by the research that has sought to compare the demographics of users with the general population. Comparing these two populations has been made relatively easy, as bike share users very often have to provide an email address when they sign up, and this has resulted in greater participation in online surveys that ask demographic questions to the bike share membership base. Much of this research has revealed common trends; users tend to be of higher average income (Fishman, Washington, Haworth, & Watson, 2015; Goodman & Cheshire, 2014) and education status (Fishman, Washington, Haworth, & Mazzei, 2014; LDA Consulting, 2017; Shaheen, Cohen, & Martin, 2013) and engaged in full- or part-time work (Woodcock, Tainio, Cheshire, O'Brien, & Goodman, 2014).

The issues examined in this chapter include income and equity issues associated with bike share, age and gender of users, compared to the general population, as well as the ethnicity of users. Some comparison in demographic characteristics between bike share users and those riding private bicycle is also offered.

5.1 Income and Equity

Several studies, from different regions of the world, have consistently found that bike share users have higher average incomes than the general population, including for Australia (Fishman et al., 2015), the United States (LDA Consulting, 2017; NACTO, 2018) and London (Goodman & Cheshire, 2014). In Melbourne, for instance, bike share members were substantially more likely to earn in excess of $104,000 per annum than the general population of Melbourne (Fishman et al., 2015). One of the reasons why bike share members tend to have higher incomes than the general population may relate to the location of docking stations. It is understandable that bike share planners focus on designing catchments intended to maximise bike share use. Naturally, this includes areas of the city with higher density and more commercial and mixed-use activity (Institute for Transportation & Development Policy, 2018). These charac-teristics are often in the core of cities, which are also home to those with higher average incomes (Currie, Stanley, & Stanley, 2007). Those work-ing in the core of cities are more likely to be engaged in the professional services economy and therefore have a higher average income, compared to those working in middle and outer suburbs.

There are several barriers that are likely to influence the demographic profile of bike share users (V. Allan, 2018, personal communication with the author – equity issues and bike share):

* Price of the system may deter lower-income groups
* Access to credit: Most systems require a credit card or debit card and a deposit
* Locations: Bike share systems have been criticised in the past for ignoring less-affluent areas of a city, instead focussing on wealthier downtown areas
* Cultural values: Bike riding may be seen by some groups as undesir-able or inappropriate as a form of transport
* Lack of suitable infrastructure: Areas with low-income communities, especially on the margins of large cities, often have less well-developed bicycle infrastructure, which results in cycling feeling unsafe, relative to areas with well-developed networks of bikes lanes and paths.

A study by Goodman and Cheshire (2014) found that users of the London bike share program were disproportionately wealthy when the program be-gan in 2010. As the program matured, however, the proportion of users from deprived areas increased from 6% to 12% between 2010 and 2013. In-terestingly, another study from London (Ogilvie & Goodman, 2012) found that 'After adjusting for the fact that those living in income-deprived areas were less likely to live close to a … docking station, registered users from deprived areas made more trips on average than those from less-deprived areas' (p. 44). The authors suggest that there may well be high latent demand for bike share in economically deprived areas. The insight from this study is that it is not so much that poorer people are not interested in bike share, but rather that they have less access it to, because of the spatial catchment of the docking stations, and perhaps also the pricing scheme. Ensuring annual sub-scription costs are within an affordable price band is suggested as one way of encouraging bike share use among low-income communities. The increase in usage fees in January 2013 did, according to Goodman and Cheshire (2014), result in a reduction in the level of *casual* use from those residing in the most economically deprived areas of London.

The growing recognition of the equity issues associated with bike share take up, especially in the United States, has resulted in the formation of programs specifically designed to address the disparity in participation. Increasing bike share membership within economically disadvantaged communities and those from minority groups has led to the formation of the *Better Bike Share Partnership*. This program has provided funding to:

- Install docking stations in underserved areas
- Develop a cash payment system for those without credit card access
- Provide discount and concession pricing schemes
- Establish education and outreach programs.

The *Better Bike Share Partnership* also undertakes research and publishes reports to help cities and bike share operators improve the equity and access to bike share schemes for all users.

5.2 Age

A number of commentators and researchers have identified that bike share users tend to be younger than the general population (Wang, Akar, & Chen, 2018). Analysts have found that older Millennials (born 1979–1988) make up most of the trips on Citi Bike in New York City (Wang et al., 2018). Research on Australia's two docked bike share programs found users to be significantly more likely to be within the 18–34 years age bracket, compared to the general population (Fishman et al., 2015). In Lyon, France, with one of the most heavily used bike share services in the world, researchers have identified that only 19% of users are older than 45 years of age. Some 56% of bike share users in Lyon are below 30 (Raux, Zoubir, & Geyik, 2017).

The fact that bike share users are generally younger than the general population may be related to these age groups being more likely to be physically capable of riding, more likely to be employed (and therefore make more trips in general) and for that work to be in the central city (where bike share is overwhelmingly located). Moreover, young adults have lower levels of car ownership (Delbosc & Currie, 2013). Finally, young adults are also less likely to have children, making bike share relatively more attractive, as using bike share with children under 15–17 is often prohibited.

5.3 Gender

Several studies have identified a relationship between gender and bike share usage. One US commentator has suggested that bike share does not have the same level of gender disparity as general cycling in North America (Goodyear, 2013), although no report details were offered allowing the reader to verify the numbers provided in the online piece. In countries with low levels of general cycling, such as the United Kingdom, the United States and Australia, between 65% and 90% of cycling trips are by men (Pucher & Buehler, 2012), whilst in strong cycling countries such as the Netherlands, women cycle more than men (Fishman, Böcker, & Helbich, 2015). Unsurprisingly, therefore, bike share programs in countries with low cycling usage have lower levels of female participation. For instance, less than 20% of trips by registered users of the London bike share program are by women (Goodman & Cheshire, 2014), though this proportion rises slightly when looking at casual users. Interestingly, female participation rises substantially for trips that start or finish in a park, possibly suggesting a desire among females to avoid motorised traffic routes in London and a recreational rather than commuting trip purpose. Previous research has found that women have a stronger preference for traffic-free riding (Johnson, Charlton, & Oxley, 2010).

A study of Australia's bike share members has found that women account for 23% and 40% of annual members in Melbourne and Brisbane, respectively, but it is not clear what accounts for the discrepancy between the two (Fishman et al., 2014). Nevertheless, the proportion of female CityCycle (Brisbane) members is greater than for private bike riding in Australia (Pucher, Greaves, & Garrard, 2010). Dublin's bike share gender split is 22% female (Murphy & Usher, 2015).

5.4 Ethnicity

The ethnicity of bike share users has been documented in some North American programs as well as in London. The results show some substantial differences between bike share users and the general population. For instance, only 3% of *Capital Bikeshare* members are African-American, compared to 8% for general bicycle riders in the D.C. area (Buck et al., 2013), despite African-Americans making up some 50% of the Washington, D.C. population (United States Census Bureau, 2013). Members of London's bike share program have been found to differ demographically from the general London population. Some 88% of respondents to a Transport for London bike share survey identified as being white (Transport for London, 2014), compared to 55% for the general London population (Office of National Statistics, 2014). As identified earlier, many bike share programs do not cover the full residential area of the city, and this may offer an explanation for the demographic biases of bike share users.

In terms of bicycle ownership, Buck et al. (2013) found only 29% of *Capital Bikeshare* members owned a bicycle, compared to 94% for general bicycle riders. A study using snowball sampling in Montreal, Canada, found those owning a bike were less frequent users of bike share

(Bachand-Marleau, Lee, & El-Geneidy, 2012). Interestingly, the same study found those possessing a driver's licence had 1.5 times greater odds of using bike share.

5.5 Differences between Bike Share Members and Private Riders

Buck et al. (2013) carried out one of the few studies that set out to specifically examine demographic differences between bike share users and other cyclists. The authors collected data on *Capital Bikeshare* users (short- and long-term subscribers) as well as regular cyclists in the same geographic area (Washington, D.C.). The authors found that in comparison to regular bicycle riders, bike share users were more likely to be female, younger and own fewer cars and bicycles. *Capital Bikeshare* users were likely to have *lower* mean household incomes compared to regular cyclists (US$81,920 compared to US$93,180). Interestingly, however, and something not reported in the Buck et al. study, median household income for the general population in the Washington, D.C. area is US$64,267 (United States Census Bureau, 2013). This suggests both bike share users and general bicycle riders have higher incomes than the general Washington, D.C. population, though it is possible response bias contributes to this difference.

In summary, bike share users are on average disproportionately of higher education and income, more likely to be male and white. The gender disparity does appear to be smaller, however, than for private bike riding.

5.6 Campus-Based Bike Share

Not all bike share programs are city-wide, open access schemes. 'Closed systems', open to only specific groups, have been operating on a large number of university campuses, often at North American universities. It is perhaps no surprise that given the demographic characteristics of bike share users discussed earlier, university campuses have been fertile ground for bike share programs. The concentration of people aged under 34, lower car ownership, and the shorter trip distances that characterise many campus environments are all predictive factors for bike share use. Despite these factors, not all campus bike share programs have been successful.

University bike share programs are generally only open to staff and students and require proof of enrolment or employment at the university before access is granted. It is perhaps because of this 'closed' type of system that many universities have opted for relatively low-tech systems. Whilst some have employed GPS, Near Field Communication and other technologies (these are discussed in Chapter 6), many are coin operated or require the bicycle to be returned to the same location.

University bike share schemes are generally small compared to general-use schemes, often with fleets of bikes less than 100 and limited docking stations on or near campus.

There are a number of reasons why a university may want to establish and operate a bike share scheme. First, university students are a key market for bicycle use. The mostly 18–24 age bracket, lower income, and often living in close proximity to the university make students highly predisposed to bike share use. International students are even more predisposed to using a bike share scheme, as they are likely to live near or on campus and less likely to have access to private transport. Providing a free or low-cost bike share scheme helps students make sustainable transport choices and improves student mobility (Fishman & Davies, 2016).

Second, universities may seek to use a bike share program to bolster their sustainability credentials. The inclusion of a bike share program is useful for marketing a university's attractiveness to potential students, showing them as supportive to environmental and social programs.

Bike share can also provide an alternative option for moving between disparate campuses. It can often be the case that large universities have relatively large geographical footprints and bike share can help to reduce travel duration between buildings at opposite ends of campus. Some universities even have a number of campuses within a close (ridable) distance. Kingston University London, for example, has only two docking stations, one at each campus, with a fleet of electric-assist bikes to undertake the 4 km trip. Similarly, campuses established in the post-Second World War era (common in North America and Australia) can be located distant from a high-capacity, high-frequency rail connection, and bike share has been used to help connect the campus to nearby public transit services. As part of the initial feasibility study for the Western Sydney University bike share program (see Fishman & Davies, 2016), a majority of student respondents to a survey said that they would find bike share useful as a *last mile* connection from the train station to the campus (a distance of 2.4 km).

Despite a large number of schemes operating within university campuses, there is a distinct lack of data and research available on their usage. It is unknown how university-based schemes perform relative to general-use schemes. One study surveyed students at Kent University on the barriers and motivators of using the university's bike share scheme (Kaplan & Knowles, 2015). The scheme was a second-generation system, offering free day-long rentals to be returned back to the station it was retrieved from. The study then undertook a series of focus groups with students. Only 12% of students surveyed had rented a bike. It was concluded that the low usage was due to the following factors:

- Lack of cycling infrastructure
- Poorly located docking stations
- Too few bikes to use the scheme regularly.

Most users were found to use the bikes for recreational purposes, rather than as transport. Three-quarters of users said the scheme had not changed their transport habits (Kaplan & Knowles, 2015).

Given the smaller scale of campus-based programs and the greater price sensitivity of a student population, universities have sometimes created a major barrier to the uptake of bike share, through their pricing structure. Overall, the university schemes tend to provide services at a significantly lower cost compared to general use bike share schemes. Many of the systems offer free usage for staff and students or very low annual memberships.

The cost of bike share on campus should generally be lower than city-wide schemes. For instance, at the largest university campus in Australia, Monash University ran a bike share program with pricing initially similar to that of a city-wide scheme. This program ran under the pricing arrangement from mid-2015 to mid-2017, with very low ridership (less than 0.2 trips per day, per bike). It was then recognised that pricing may be contributing to low ridership and the scheme was overhauled, resulting in the elimination of user fees. The impact on ridership was dramatic, with an approximately 20-fold increase in ridership (to around four trips per day per bike during the semester), based on data automatically collected on ridership (A. Majokah, 2018, personal communication, Monash Bike Share).

Similarly, when a scheme starts free and then a price is introduced, ridership can decrease, sometimes dramatically. For instance, a bike share program run at the University of South Florida introduced pricing after initially being free, and this led to ridership dropping from over ten trips per day, per bike, to just under one trip per day, per bike (A. Majokah, 2018, personal communication, Monash Bike Share). It is questionable whether the little revenue returned from the introduction of a fee outweighs the substantial drop in usage that accompanies the introduction of a user fee.

Overall, it is clear that campus bike share is strengthened by the underlying demographics that characterise many university campuses. The performance of these schemes can be enhanced through low or no cost pricing structures, enhanced bicycle infrastructure and catchments that extend beyond the campus itself to key transport hubs, nearby shops and services.

References

Bachand-Marleau, J., Lee, B. H. Y., & El-Geneidy, A. M. (2012). Better understanding of factors influencing likelihood of using shared bicycle systems and frequency of use. *Transportation Research Record: Journal of the Transportation Research Board, 2314*, 66–71. doi:10.3141/2314-09

Buck, D., Buehler, R., Happ, P., Rawls, B., Chung, P. P., & Borecki, N. (2013). Are bikeshare users different from regular cyclists? *Transportation Research Record: Journal of the Transportation Research Board, 2387*(1), 112–119.

Currie, G., Stanley, J., & Stanley, J. (2007). *No Way to Go: Transport and Social Disadvantage in Australian Communities.* Melbourne: Monash University ePress.

Delbosc, A., & Currie, G. (2013). Causes of youth licensing decline: A synthesis of evidence. *Transport Reviews, 33*(3), 271–290. doi:10.1080/01441647.2013.801929

Fishman, E., Böcker, L., & Helbich, M. (2015). Adult active transport in the Netherlands: An analysis of its contribution to physical activity requirements. *PloS ONE, 10*(4), e0121871. doi:10.1371/journal.pone.0121871

Fishman, E., & Davies, L. (2016). Bike Share at Western Sydney University Parramatta. Retrieved from Melbourne: https://sensibletransport.org.au/project/western-sydney-university-bike-share-feasibility-study/

Fishman, E., Washington, S., Haworth, N., & Mazzei, A. (2014). Barriers to bikesharing: An analysis from Melbourne and Brisbane. *Journal of Transport Geography, 41,* 325–337.

Fishman, E., Washington, S., Haworth, N., & Watson, A. (2015). Factors influencing bike share membership: An analysis of Melbourne and Brisbane. *Transportation Research Part A, 71,* 17–30. doi:10.1016/j.tra.2014.10.021

Goodman, A., & Cheshire, J. (2014). Inequalities in the London bicycle sharing system revisited: Impacts of extending the scheme to poorer areas but then doubling prices. *Journal of Transport Geography, 41,* 272–279. doi: 10.1016/j.jtrangeo.2014.04.004

Goodyear, S. (2013). Bike-share is key to closing the cycling gender gap. *The Atlantic Monthly.* Retrieved from http://www.theatlanticcities.com/commute/2013/08/bike-share-may-be-one-key-closing-cycling-gender-gap/6580/

Institute for Transportation & Development Policy. (2018). The Bikeshare Planning Guide. Retrieved from New York: https://www.itdp.org/publication/the-bike-share-planning-guide/

Johnson, M., Charlton, J., & Oxley, J. (2010). The application of a naturalistic driving method to investigate on-road cyclist behaviour: A feasibility study. *Road & Transport Research: A Journal of Australian and New Zealand Research and Practice, 19*(2), 32–41.

Kaplan, D. H., & Knowles, M. J. (2015). Developing a next-generation campus bike-share program: Examining demand and supply factors. *Planning for Higher Education, 44*(1), 63–75.

LDA Consulting. (2017). 2016 Capital Bikeshare Member Survey Report. Retrieved from Washington, DC: https://d21xlh2maitm24.cloudfront.net/wdc/Capital-Bikeshare_2016MemberSurvey_Executive-Summary.pdf?mtime=20170303165533

Lewis, T. (2011). Has London's cycle hire scheme been a capital idea? *Guardian* Retrieved from http://www.guardian.co.uk/uk/bike-blog/2011/jul/10/boris-bikes-hire-scheme-london?commentpage=all#start-of-comments

Murphy, E., & Usher, J. (2015). The role of bicycle-sharing in the city: Analysis of the Irish experience. *International Journal of Sustainable Transportation, 9*(2). doi:10.1080/15568318.2012.748855

NACTO. (2018). Bike Share in the U.S. 2017. Retrieved from https://nacto.org/bike-share-statistics-2017/

Office of National Statistics. (2014). National Statistics from United Kingdom Government https://www.gov.uk/government/statistics/announcements

Ogilvie, D., & Goodman, A. (2012). Inequities in usage of a public bicycle sharing scheme: Socio-demographic predictors of uptake and usage of the London (UK) cycle hire scheme. *Preventive Medicine, 55*(1), 40–45. doi:10.1016/j.ypmed.2012.05.002

Pucher, J., & Buehler, R. (2012). *City Cycling.* Cambridge, MA: MIT Press.

Pucher, J., Greaves, S., & Garrard, J. (2010). Cycling down under: A comparative analysis of bicycling trends and policies in Sydney and Melbourne. *Journal of Transport Geography, 19*(2), 332–345.

Raux, C., Zoubir, A., & Geyik, M. (2017). Who are bike sharing schemes members and do they travel differently? The case of Lyon's "Vélo'v" scheme. *Transportation Research Part A, 106*, 350–363.

Shaheen, S., Cohen, A. P., & Martin, E. W. (2013). Public bikesharing in North America: Early operator understanding and emerging trends. *Transportation Research Record: Journal of the Transportation Research Board, 2387*, 83–92. doi:10.3141/2387-10

Transport for London. (2014). Barclays Cycle Hire Customer Satisfaction and Usage Survey: Members Only. Retrieved from London: http://www.tfl.gov.uk/cdn/static/cms/documents/barclays-cycle-hire-css-and-usage-members-q3-2013-14.pdf

United States Census Bureau. (2013). State and Country QuickFacts. Retrieved from http://quickfacts.census.gov/qfd/states/11000.html

Wang, K., Akar, G., & Chen, Y.-J. (2018). Bike sharing differences among millennials, Gen Xers, and baby boomers: Lessons learnt from New York City's bike share. *Transportation Research Part A: Policy and Practice, 116*, 1–14. doi: 10.1016/j.tra.2018.06.001

Woodcock, J., Tainio, M., Cheshire, J., O'Brien, O., & Goodman, A. (2014). Health effects of the London bicycle sharing system: Health impact modelling study. *BMJ, 348.* doi:10.1136/bmj.g425

6 Bike Share Innovation and Technologies

Technology has been central to the development of modern bike share programs (Fishman, 2016). As identified earlier, technology was crucial to overcoming the challenge of misuse that led to the demise of the first-generation bike share program (Amsterdam's *White Bikes*). Since that time, the technology underpinning bike share programs has grown increasingly sophisticated, which has enhanced both the user experience, as well as the capacity of operators to manage the bicycle fleet.

The coin-operated systems like that launched in Copenhagen in the 1990s were certainly an advance from a technological perspective, but, as previously mentioned, the anonymity of the rider still meant that too many bikes were stolen or vandalised (DeMaio, 2009). Bike share misuse was a key motivation for bike share operators to integrate technology that identified the rider, which deterred people from stealing or damaging bikes. A big advance in bike share came with the credit card, which could easily be used to act as both a form of security (in case of damage or theft) and payment for usage. Without the widespread adoption of universal credit cards, it is difficult to see how bike share's growth would have eventuated.

The most recent technological advance in bike share has been the advent of digitally connected, smartphone accessible bike share (referred to throughout this book as *dockless* bike share). By removing the need for a physical dock, these systems have dramatically reduced the cost associated with bike share setup, and many private-sector operators now provide large-scale systems without any direct government subsidy. It is also now commonplace for multiple dockless bike share providers to be operating within the same city. In Beijing for example, there are no less than 15 companies offering dockless bike share services. As this chapter will demonstrate, whilst the massive scale of these dockless systems have made tangle inroads to improving transport sustainability (e.g., the bike mode share of Beijing rose from 5% to 12% according to operator Mobike), these systems have also proved a challenge for government agencies responsible for public realm management, particularly in relation to parking issues. Parking issues associated with dockless bike share are discussed in Chapter 7.

This chapter introduces some of the different types of bike share systems and technologies currently on the market and concludes with a brief discussion of the key trends that are likely to impact on bike share in the future.

6.1 Smart Dock, Dumb Bike

The third-generation bike share systems were really the breakthrough technology that spurred much of bike share's growth between 2005 and 2013. These systems have been characterised by some as *smart dock, dumb bike*. The 'brains' of the system are in the docking stations themselves, leaving the bicycle largely free of digital technology. Generally through the use of Radio Frequency Identification tags, or RFID for short (described below), a system operator is able to track bikes whenever a bike is removed or returned to a docking station. In these systems, docking stations can either be fixed into the ground (e.g., Brisbane, Paris and London), or modular and flexible (e.g., Melbourne, New York City, Washington, D.C.). The general trend is for cities that have launched a bike share program since 2010–2011 to opt for modular designs with solar power, to avoid additional installation costs.

6.2 Dumb Dock, Smart Bike

In the past 3–5 years, a new bike share system has emerged that generally uses GPS and other technology (described below) on the bike itself, with technologically intensive docking stations being replaced by relatively ordinary bike parking hoops (or simply space on the pavement) in order to park stationary bikes. In many of these systems (e.g., see Uber's *JUMP*), the bicycle's location is monitored constantly through the use of on-board, solar-powered GPS. This provides both the operator and user with real-time bicycle tracking. As will be described later in this chapter, and in Chapter 7, some dockless bike share suppliers rely on the GPS capabilities of the riders' smartphone, rather than a bike-integrated GPS. This can lead to a lack of real-time information, should the bicycle be moved whilst still locked (to itself).

Affordable GPS, combined with the ubiquity of the smartphone has made it possible to operate these systems without the need for any fixed points to lock the bicycle. These 'floating systems', in which users locate bicycles through their smartphone are becoming increasingly popular. Mobike, one of the largest suppliers of dockless bike share, developed by a former Uber employee has adopted this model and shares some of the intuitive user interface characteristics that have helped to make Uber a household name in a short space of time. A typical image of a dockless bike share bike is shown in Figure 6.1, in which all the technology is positioned on the bike itself, integrated with a 'horseshoe' lock positioned to hold the rear wheel.

The original version of the *dumb dock, smart bike* model, developed by SocialBicycles in NYC is shown in Figure 6.2. One key advantage of this

Figure 6.1 Dockless bike share.
Source: Mobike.

approach is the integration of a mechanism that allows the bicycle to be locked to a fixed structure, rather than just being able to be locked to itself. A major benefit of this design is that it reduces the opportunity for misuse that has characterised dockless bike share systems that only lock the bicycle to itself. When a bicycle is locked only to itself, opportunities for theft and vandalism are created.

One benefit of the older, 'smart dock, dumb bike' system is it provides certainty to users and operators. The locations in which bikes can be picked up and dropped off are fixed. However, one disadvantage of the 'smart dock, dumb bike' model is that these docks can be overloaded or emptied and require physical rebalancing, and this comes at a substantial cost to operators, as well as users (when stations become either 100% full or empty).

The 'smart bike, dumb dock' system does not completely avoid the rebalancing issue, as bikes can become clustered around some areas, whilst other parts of the city may be devoid of bikes. It would appear that having the option to lock a bike to itself and end the rental period (as is possible in most *smart bike* systems is a distinct advantage). Trying to return a bike within a docked system and finding all the slots full is one of the main causes of frustration with the London bike share program, for instance (Transport for London, 2018). Some 'smart bike, dumb dock' operators allow users to reserve bikes in advance (through a smartphone App), reducing the inconvenience of not being able to find an available bike.

The rise of electric assist bike share bikes is discussed in Section 6.2.6 and is one of the most exciting advances in bike share technology. One of the implications of this development for the question of docked or dockless

Figure 6.2 Smart bike.
Source: JUMP.

bike share is that the charging of the battery is made considerably more complex (though not impossible) without docks. The docks typically form part of the charging infrastructure.

The following provides an overview of some of the key technologies that have become important components of modern bike share programs.

6.2.1 Radio Frequency Identification

Third-generation bike share programs, which accounted for the vast majority of the bike share programs globally until 2016, rely on the use of RFID tags to allow users to unlock and return bicycles into docking stations. Operators are also able to remotely detect the presence of each bike when it is parked at a docking station. This has created rich datasets that have enabled researchers to produce detailed geospatial visualisations of bike share activity (e.g., see Beecham & Wood, 2014; O'Brien, 2014; O'Brien, Cheshire, & Batty, 2014). A new row is created in an automatically generated spreadsheet each time a bicycle is removed, including the time of its removal, as well as the time and location the bicycle was returned (usually to a different docking station). This has created practical visualisations of bike share system usage, which can be useful both for bike share operators, as well as researchers seeking to identify usage patterns.

The benefits of using RFIDs are that they are affordable, proven, and provide automated data on usage. The limitations of RFIDs are that they are only able to provide information when bicycles interact with the docking stations (removed or returned) and do not provide any information whilst the bicycle is actually in use (i.e., what route the bicycle has taken).[1]

6.2.2 GPS and Dockless Systems

As of mid-2019, GPS has become widespread across bike share systems. GPS is now seen as a relatively affordable method to track bicycles in real time and has become central to the global expansion of dockless bike share. Many programs introduced over the last few years include GPS technology within the bicycles, and some older programs that are in the process of fleet renewal have taken the opportunity of more affordable GPS to include this technology within its updated fleet of bicycles (e.g., London). Unlike RFID technology described earlier, GPS enables operators (and users) to be able to track the route bicycles travel. One of the functions that has attracted bike share suppliers/operators to GPS is the *route finding* function that becomes possible with GPS capabilities. GPS provides the potential for local businesses to partner with bike share operators, to offer specials/discount offers to riders, based on their proximity to the business.

Apart from the obvious security benefits, GPS may assist bike share operators by providing a 'geo-fence', detecting when a bicycle has moved outside a given area. Operators may also use GPS to assist with the challenging task of re-distributing bicycles across their fleet via the use of real-time tracking. Users may benefit by enhanced real-time information on bicycle availability. The automated data collection offered through GPS provides new opportunities for data analysis, which may not only be useful for bike share operators to understand how their system is being used but also from a wider transport planning perspective. Openly available GeoJSON data files may assist governments plan and evaluate bicycle route usage and effectiveness. These geographic datasets will help build on the impressive work that has begun using start and end docking station locations provided by non-GPS bike share programs (e.g., see Beecham & Wood, 2014; Romanillos, Zaltz Austwick, Ettema, & De Kruijf, 2015; Zaltz Austwick, O'Brien, Strano, & Viana, 2013).

Integrating a bike share system with GPS does, however, increase the costs to the operator, in the form of unit costs, as well as monthly data charges. On balance, the benefit of GPS (data on route selection, enhanced security and rebalancing insights) is likely to outweigh costs, as the technology becomes more affordable. The wayfinding potential of a GPS-integrated bike share system is of particular relevance to those cities in which protected bicycle lanes and paths are not ubiquitous (i.e., most cities). Given the limitations of the current bicycle infrastructure network in many cities and the need to maximise safety outcomes for road users, *digital wayfinding* is likely to be an important emerging trend for bike share cities in the future and is discussed below.

6.2.3 Digital Wayfinding

The introduction of GPS-integrated bike share fleets provides a platform for a number of wayfinding technologies that seek to make bike share safer and more convenient. One example is *Smart Halo*, which provides route-finding functions (among others) to help riders find the quickest or safest route between two points. A number of bike share hardware manufacturers are now working with companies like *Smart Halo*, to integrate these GPS-embedded wayfinding interfaces to their bikes.

In cities in which it is anticipated there will be a strong tourist/visitor market, digital wayfinding may be especially useful, as many of these visitors will be unfamiliar with the city's bicycle infrastructure. Previous research suggests that for those unfamiliar with public transport, wayfinding uncertainty can lead to anxiety and sometimes trip suppression (Schmitt, Currie, & Delbosc, 2015) so it may be that wayfinding information on bike share would improve customer experience and attract higher utilisation. Recognising that some people will have a preference for using their own smartphone to assist with navigation, the newly designed *JUMP* bicycles (e-assist), as well as those provided by LIME include a handlebar-mounted smartphone holder.

6.2.4 Near Field Communication

Near Field Communication (NFC) is a form of wireless data transfer that detects and then facilitates compatible devices within 5 cm to communicate directly, without using the Internet. NFC is increasingly being used in a wide range of applications, such as in store, contactless payment (e.g., PayPass), as well as public transport mobile ticketing (e.g., Portland's *Mobile Tickets* and Chicago's *Ventra Mobile App*). *Apple Pay* and *Google Wallet* use NFC to enable subscribers to pay using their smartphone. Significant potential exists for bike share to use NFC to make accessing bicycles easier than it was for older, third-generation, docked bike share programs in which a physical 'fob' (access key) was required. Potential users could use their smartphone (providing it has NFC functionality) to pay for and release bicycles, lowering the 'friction' that can sometimes prevent those who have not yet used bike share to begin the process. Moreover, for existing users, a smartphone could replace the current fob annual members presently require to access some systems. It is the author's understanding that most large bike share operators are currently working to make their systems smartphone accessible, through the use of NFC.

The French company *Smoove*, which provides bikes for the Helsinki and Vancouver bike share programs (and most recently Paris's *Velib* system), provides NFC technology on a panel located at the centre of the handlebars (shown in Figure 6.3).

A number of companies are utilising the capabilities offered by NFC and the ubiquity of the smartphone to offer apps that provide an interface for riders to complete the sign up process, from start to finish. London's new App has this capability, and the Canadian company *PBSC Urban Solutions* offers this function in the cities using its technology.

Figure 6.3 Customer interface provided on Smoove bikes.
Source: Smoove.

6.2.5 QR Codes

The rapid introduction of dockless bike share, documented herein, would not have been possible without a seamless method of enabling a prospective user to sign up very quickly. In most cases, the dockless bike share industry has relied on QR (Quick Reponses) Codes to do this. QR Codes are readable via smartphone and link the user to a website or App and can be found on several places on a typical dockless bike share bike. Once signed up, a user simply scans the QR Code on the bike they wish to ride, automatically unlocking the horseshoe lock at the rear wheel. There have been some instances of misuse of QR Codes within bike share, including rival companies scratching out the QR Codes on the bikes of competing firms. Somewhat more worrying, people have malevolently replaced genuine bike share QR Codes with fraudulent ones, directing the unsuspecting user to a site not related to bike share.

6.2.6 E-bikes and Bike Share

The growth of bike share noted earlier has coincided with a similarly rapid growth in e-bike performance, affordability and usage (Fishman & Cherry, 2015). In recent years, a number of cities have launched bike share programs that offer electric assistance, known as pedelecs (e-bike share). These cities include Copenhagen and Madrid, as well as a growing number of smaller Italian and Spanish cities. Germany and Japan have begun e-bike share programs. Barcelona and Milan recently introduced e-bikes as part of their existing bike share programs. A university-based e-bike share program has been trialled in the United States (Langford, Cherry, Yoon, Worley, & Smith, 2013). The Paris bike share program, Velib (the largest in Europe), renewed their fleet of bicycles in January 2018, and around 30% of the bicycles are electric assist.

Birmingham, Alabama launched a system that uses a combination of conventional and electric assist bike share bikes. The electric assist bikes are ridden *three times* as much as the conventional bicycles (Bewegen Technologies, Inc., 2016). A docking station in the Birmingham, Alabama system is shown in Figure 6.4 and uses the solar panels to charge the batteries that power the electric bicycles.

Where direct sunlight is not available (e.g., in downtown areas due to shading from buildings), the manufacturers are able to tap into the closest light post, to provide the energy to charge the batteries.

Research on private e-bike riding has shown that trip distances are around 50% longer (than regular bike trips), people make more frequent trips, and that these trips are more likely to be used as a replacement for motor vehicle trips (Cairns, Behrendt, Raffo, Beaumont, & Kiefer, 2017; Fyhri & Fearnley, 2015; Fyhri, Sundfer, & Weber, 2016). The reason this

Figure 6.4 Electric assist bike share in Birmingham, Alabama.
Source: Bewegen Technologies, Inc.

is important is because when electric assist technology is offered as a part of a bike share system, it widens the appeal of bike share, and increases both trip distance and frequency. This serves to bolster many of the benefits of bike share outlined in Chapter 4.

E-bike share offers the potential to increase the attractiveness of bike share to those who may not have previously seen it as an option. Some may even be attracted to use an e-bike in a bike share system just to experience the novelty of using an e-bike. Longer trips, challenging topography, excessive heat and other factors associated with physical exertion can act as barriers to transport cycling generally (Heinen, van Wee, & Maat, 2010), as well as bike share. Furthermore, as described in Box 8.2, many bike share cities have experienced re-balancing issues associated with the city's topography. It is typical for users to ride downhill and show a reluctance to return bicycles to stations located at a higher elevation (Jurdak, 2013). E-bikes may assist in reducing this flow imbalance. Some cities (e.g., Brisbane) have avoided placing docking stations in hilly suburbs, on the assumption that it will cause redistribution issues. The inclusion of e-bikes into a bike share system gives planners the freedom to develop a catchment area without being constrained by a city's topographical challenges.

In conclusion, a range of technologies have served to enhance both the user experience and operational efficiency of bike share. Technology was central to the security and payment mechanisms that enabled third-generation bike share to flourish, without the frequent theft, vandalism and other forms of misuse that led to the demise of earlier generations of bike share. Widespread smartphone adoption and GPS has opened up additional possibilities for bike share, including real-time tracking, and mobile first sign up, especially through the use of QR Codes. The technological developments described in this chapter have all acted to make the experience of riding a bike share bike for the first time as fast and convenient as possible. Importantly, these technologies have made the roll out of bike share cheaper than it was when docking stations were required, which has resulted in larger schemes, and there are most certainly cities with bike share now that would not have seen a scheme introduced, had it not been for the availability of these new technologies. At the time of writing, e-bike share is just beginning to take off, and it is these authors view that in a decade from now, it is possible that the majority of bike share systems will at least have a proportion of their fleet as e-assist bicycles, and many programs will be made up entirely of e-assist bikes.

Note

1 This could be a potentially useful source of data to government, particularly in terms of route choice information and implications for future infrastructure provision.

References

Beecham, R., & Wood, J. (2014). Characterising group-cycling journeys using interactive graphics. *Transportation Research Part C: Emerging Technologies, 47,* 194–206. doi: 10.1016/j.trc.2014.03.007

Bewegen Technologies, Inc. (2016, 16th December). Discussion between Marc Delesclefs (Bewegen) and Elliot Fishman (Institute for Sensible Transport).

Cairns, S., Behrendt, F., Raffo, D., Beaumont, C., & Kiefer, C. (2017). Electrically-assisted bikes: Potential impacts on travel behaviour. *Transportation Research Part A: Policy and Practice, 103,* 327–342. doi: 10.1016/j.tra.2017.03.007

DeMaio, P. (2009). Bike-sharing: History, impacts, models of provision, & future. *Journal of Public Transportation, 12*(4), 41–56.

Fishman, E. (2016). Cycling as transport. *Transport Reviews, 36*(1), 1–8. doi:10.10 80/01441647.2015.1114271

Fishman, E., & Cherry, C. (2015). E-bikes in the mainstream: Reviewing a decade of research. *Transport Reviews,* 1–20. doi:10.1080/01441647.2015.1069907

Fyhri, A., & Fearnley, N. (2015). Effects of e-bikes on bicycle use and mode share. *Transportation Research Part D: Transport and Environment, 36,* 45–52. doi: 10.1016/j.trd.2015.02.005

Fyhri, A., Sundfer, H. B., & Weber, C. (2016). Effect of Subvention Program for E-bikes in Oslo on Bicycle Use, Transport Distribution and CO2 Emissions. Retrieved from Oslo: https://www.toi.no/getfile.php/1343460/Publikasjoner/T%C3%98I%20rapporter/2016/1498-2016/1498-2016_Summary.pdf

Heinen, E., van Wee, B., & Maat, K. (2010). Commuting by bicycle: An overview of the literature. *Transport Reviews, 30*(1), 59–96. doi:10.1080/01441640903187001

Jurdak, R. (2013). The impact of cost and network topology on urban mobility: A study of public bicycle usage in 2 U.S. cities. *PloS ONE, 8*(11), e79396.

Langford, B. C., Cherry, C., Yoon, T., Worley, S., & Smith, D. (2013). North America's first E-bikeshare. *Transportation Research Record: Journal of the Transportation Research Board, 2387*(1), 120–128.

O'Brien, O. (2014). Bike Share Map. Retrieved from http://bikes.oobrien.com/

O'Brien, O., Cheshire, J., & Batty, M. (2014). Mining bicycle sharing data for generating insights into sustainable transport systems. *Journal of Transport Geography, 34,* 262–273. doi:10.1016/j.jtrangeo.2013.06.007

Romanillos, G., Zaltz Austwick, M., Ettema, D., & De Kruijf, J. (2015). Big data and cycling. *Transport Reviews,* 1–20. doi:10.1080/01441647.2015.1084067

Schmitt, L., Currie, G., & Delbosc, A. (2015). Lost in transit? Unfamiliar public transport travel explored using a journey planner web survey. *Transportation, 42*(1), 101–122. doi:10.1007/s11116-014-9529-2

Transport for London. (2018). Santander Cycles Customer Satisfaction and Usage Survey Casual Users Only: Quarter 2 2017/18. Retrieved from London: http://content.tfl.gov.uk/santander-cycles-casuals-css-q2-2017-18.pdf

Zaltz Austwick, M., O'Brien, O., Strano, E., & Viana, M. (2013). The Structure of Spatial Networks and Communities in Bicycle Sharing Systems. *PloS ONE, 8*(9), e74685.

7 The Challenges of Dockless Bike Share Parking

7.1 Introduction

As previously discussed, dockless bike share is rapidly emerging in cities around the world. The introduction of these 'floating' systems present opportunities for large-scale bike share without the level of government expenditure required for some docked bike share systems (Institute for Transportation & Development Policy, 2018). The rapid introduction of large dockless bike share programs during the 2015–2018 period became a highly contentious issue in cities around the world. The issue was most pronounced in Chinese cities, with hundreds of thousands of bikes, and in some cases, *millions* of bikes introduced into a city, often with little or no notice. This created major issues in terms of footpath accessibility and the use of the public realm for bike storage. The lack of docking locations or suitable places to park these large numbers of bicycles resulted in a multitude of public nuisance issues. In many cases, again, especially in China, the size of the system was larger than the demand for bike share, and in the few years since their initial launch, many dockless bike share programs have had to scale back their overall fleet size, as a direct result of the public (and government) backlash from what was generally seen as *litter* rather than a crucial part of the transport system.

Many cities in North America have introduced permit systems and caps on the maximum number of bicycles any one dockless operator is able to introduce (Yanocha, 2018).

When assessing the parking-related issues associated with large-scale dockless bike share, it is worth noting the three elements of any transport mode, introduced in Chapter 1. Dockless bike share only provides one of these three elements, namely the bicycle. The *terminal capacity* (where bicycles are parked) or *rights of way* (where bicycles travel) are not included as part of the system and must be provided, often by another entity (like a local government). The public nuisance and controversy associated with dockless bike share identified at the beginning of this chapter is in essence, a failure to recognise the need to integrate *terminal capacity* into the bike share model. This chapter discusses the issues associated with the parking of dockless bike share bikes and opportunities to minimise the negative impact they can have on public realm outcomes.

In mid-2017, due to the rapid advancement of dockless bike share systems in hundreds of cities across the globe, a study was conducted on the parking-related issues associated with dockless bike share (see Fishman, 2017). In the 18 months since this investigation was undertaken, a number of dockless bike share firms have since abandoned the market. For instance, of the five companies operating dockless bike share in Sydney, Australia, only one continues to operate (Mobike), and at a much smaller scale than when entering the market. A number of cities, including Beijing, have seen a retraction in the scale of dockless bike share operations, due primarily to government and public concerns regarding the space consumed by masses of parked (and sometimes discarded bikes). The following provides a distillation of the issues to emerge from a 2017 global investigation of parking-related issues associated with dockless bikes (Fishman, 2017). This investigation included interviews with local government officials charged with the responsibility of managing issues associated with dockless bike share, as well as a Chinese official responsible for developing a national policy regarding dockless bike share. These interviews were conducted with officials located in London, Manchester, Amsterdam, Beijing, Seattle, Melbourne and Sydney.

7.1.1 Poor Engagement with Government Agencies

City officials revealed that little or no communication had been initiated by dockless bike share operators prior to the launch of dockless bike share. This was consistent across the cities included in the investigation. The communication since launch was described by city officials as sporadic and inconsistent. Many of the dockless bike share providers took an approach not dissimilar to Uber when it too was a fledgling transport platform, in that they began their service and asked for permission later. This was not always the case, and there are certainly operators who more consistently approach city governments in a consultative manner, prior to launch (e.g., Mobike in Manchester, UK). However, in most cases, including London, Amsterdam and Melbourne, bikes often 'appeared' without communication with city officials. When dockless bike share had arrived at the English capital, the bikes were deployed directly at the slots of the long-standing Santander (docked) Cycle Hire program run by Transport for London, to the frustration of their operator.

7.1.2 Public Amenity and Access Issues

Perhaps the most significant concern that has accompanied the rise of dockless bike share has been access issues caused by inappropriately parked (or dumped) bicycles. Clusters of bikes have caused issues for those with a disability, blocked public transport access, overwhelmed existing bicycle parking and reduced the amenity of the streetscape. In many cases, especially in central city areas, the number of bikes clustering together is well beyond demand or the natural carrying capacity of the footpath in which they have been deployed.

Fallen bikes have caused safety issues and reduced the visual attractiveness of the street. Some large dockless bike share companies do not include technology capable of remotely detecting when a bicycle is no longer upright, meaning a bicycle may remain in a fallen position for extended periods. Figure 7.1 shows a typical scene following a windy day in Melbourne, where the bicycle stand is insufficient to maintain the bicycles in an upright position.

As mentioned earlier, some suppliers do not include tracing technology on the bicycle itself. The lack of GPS integration means that some companies are unable to detect bicycles that have been moved whilst still locked. This has reduced their ability to identify bicycles that have been dumped (e.g., left in parkland and waterways). In cities with waterways, this can be a significant problem, with one provider in Melbourne, Australia having a significant proportion of their fleet thrown into the city's main river.

Another issue raised by some local government officials relates to the equity or fairness of allowing a commercial provider to operate within the public realm without paying a fee (as café or other businesses may

Figure 7.1 Fallen dockless bikes, Melbourne.
Source: Institute for Sensible Transport.

be required to do). Existing businesses (e.g., restaurants) have expressed frustration with the dockless bike share industry that they must accord with regulations that are not applied to dockless bike share. This has begun to change and during 2017 and 2018, cities, especially in North American (e.g., Seattle), began requiring a permitting fee, on a per bicycle basis (Yanocha, 2018). In some cases, this fee was reimbursed if the operator satisfied all of their obligations with regard to maintenance, customer service and other conditions of the contract/agreement.

7.1.3 Quality of Bike

A number of local governments have expressed concern regarding the quality of bike provided by dockless bike share companies. Poor-quality componentry has reduced ride quality and usability. As touched on earlier, the quality of the stand has been so poor in some instances that even moderately strong wind can cause the bicycle to fall. This is particularly a problem when multiple bicycles are parked close to one another, as it creates a 'domino effect'. Docked bike share hardware is often made to be resistant to the rigours of being exposed to the elements (both natural and human) and can be substantially stronger and vandal resistant than private bicycles. Some dockless bike manufacturers have not taken this approach, and their fleet can suffer the impacts of use (both proper and improper), with large proportions of the fleet unusable.

7.2 Recommended Responses for Cities Seeking to Integrate Dockless Bike Share

The rise of the commercial dockless bike share sector has occurred faster than government regulation, and this gap has contributed to the parking issues described above. The negative impacts of dockless bike share do not, however, mean that they should be discouraged. For many cities, dockless bike share may be the only option available, due to a lack of funds for more expensive docked bike share. As will be described in subsequent chapters of this book, each bike within a docked bike share system can cost between $6,000 and $10,000, which can be seen as too expensive for many cities, or can result in a system too small to achieve its objectives. Moreover, the freedom of being able to end a trip as close as possible to the final destination, without having to look for a fixed docking station makes dockless bike share more convenient in some instances.

The following set of recommended policy responses are designed for cities interested in adopting dockless bike share whilst minimising some of the parking problems that have been described above.

7.2.1 Developing a Memorandum of Understanding or Permit Requirement Procedure

Some cities (e.g., Seattle, San Francisco) have developed a permit application process that prospective bike share suppliers/operators must satisfy in order to be considered as a registered bike share supplier (Yanocha, 2018). In some cases, city governments require an annual, per bike payment to be made, and these funds are often intended to be spent on bicycle-related infrastructure and management. This is a stark reversal of docked bike share, which in many cases required governments to pay the operator substantial funds to provide a full-service bike share system for their city.

The permit application procedure should stipulate clear, measurable requirements suppliers/operators must meet in order to maintain their licence to operate. This could include the following:

- Density of bicycle supply, to ensure deployment operations do not overwhelm the ability of the public realm to absorb new bicycles. In some cities, private operations teams have simply deployed an excessive number of bicycles in one small defined area, and this has led to the city government impounding the bicycles.

  Determining the appropriate density of bicycles is likely to require a data-driven approach, in which several Census-collected variables are mapped to create a composite index of *demand for bike share parking*. This is likely to include commercial and residential density, as well as proximity to major public transport nodes and entertainment areas. The output might be a heat map, showing how forecast demand for parking varies.

- Direct lines of communication between city authorities and bike share operators. A special hotline/email address may need to be maintained to ensure government agencies are able to directly contact the bike share operator. In the past, the lack of such a service has meant that important issues have not been adequately dealt with by the bike share operator. Contact details, including a telephone number and email address, could also be included on bikes, allowing members of the public (including those who are not part of the scheme) to easily contact the operator to inform them about any issues (e.g., damaged or inappropriately parked bicycles).

- Levies: Cities should consider whether it would assist them to have bike share operators pay a per bike levy to operate in their city. This annual fee may help cover the cost associated with managing the impacts of bike share operators, and for the installation of new bicycle parking hoops and/or special dockless bike parking areas.

More specific requirements may also need to be developed as part of the Memorandum of Understanding (MOU)/Permit process, including the following:

- Number of bicycles to be deployed.
- Consideration of vulnerable road users, such as pedestrians, disabled people and those who are visually or hearing impaired.
- Operational processes for customers to easily report damaged bicycles and agreed response times.
- Minimum standards for the appropriate parking of bicycles and the methods via which these will be communicated with riders (e.g., via the App, short video clip).
- Time period for the removal of bicycles reported as being parked inappropriately, dumped or otherwise inoperable/unsafe. The response time should be proportional to the severity of the issue. For instance, a bicycle blocking an emergency exist will need to be removed faster than a bicycle inappropriately parked but not posing a safety risk.
- Dormant bicycles: Once a bicycle has remained in the same location for a certain period of time (e.g., seven days), the operator will be required to relocate the bicycle to an area of higher demand.
- Liaison and agreement between bike share provider and city authority/ies regarding zones that are suitable/not suitable for parking of dockless bikes. These zones need to be integrated with government and dockless bike share providers GIS software so that areas not suitable for the parking of dockless bike are made clear. This can then be communicated to riders via the App, whereby a rider trying to end a trip in a prohibited zone will be sent a notification of the closest place they are able to park the bicycle.
- Technical and operational capability to monitor the location of all bicycles in the fleet, in real time. The operator must be able to show the responsible authority that it has the capability to track their fleet at all times, both when the bicycles are in use, and stationary. In some cases, cities may wish to create data sharing agreements in which the operator provides de-personalised trip data, to see trip beginning and end points, as well as route choices. This may be used by city planners when deciding locations for bicycle infrastructure, both in terms of bicycle lanes/paths, as well as places for bicycle parking corrals, when areas of high parking demand have been detected.
- Capability to detect when a bicycle is no longer in an upright position and a procedure for sending support staff to remedy.
- Capability of operator to maintain a balanced fleet of bicycles. An objective metric will need to be created to ensure the definition of *balanced* is understood by all parties.

At the time of writing, Seattle,[1] San Francisco,[2] London[3] and central parts of Melbourne[4] and Sydney[5] have developed MOU/permit style requirements or codes of conduct, and it is understood that many more cities are currently in the process of drafting similar regulations.

7.2.2 Creating Space to Park Bikes

As mentioned earlier, transport systems are composed of three elements (see Section 1.4) and one of these three elements, namely; *terminal capacity* (i.e., parking) is most appropriately provided by government. In the short history of dockless bike share, the most consistently successful measure to reduce parking-related issues has been the designation of specially created areas to park dockless bikes (corrals). China and some other parts of Asia, due in part to the greater length of time dockless bike share has operated, have created designated bike parking areas, often accompanied by information totems that offer information on how to use the service (see Figure 7.2).

The totem can be used to maximise awareness of how to use the bike share scheme. In terms of information provision, a map of the area is provided, showing current location, the bicycle network and other priority bike parking areas. In other areas, a minimalist approach is suggested, directing people to a website via a QR code and instructions on how to download the App.

A promotional clip (~30-second video) may need to be developed by government, in conjunction with bike share operators, highlighting how to use dockless bike share appropriately, particularly in terms of parking

Figure 7.2 Shanghai dockless bike share parking. Source: Mobike.

Figure 7.3 London's approach to creating designated parking.
Source: Ofo.

behaviour. This can be promoted using social media platforms, as well as via the bike share Apps and websites.

These dockless bike share parking corrals should be located at key activity centres, such as shopping precincts, public transport hubs and other areas where demand is expected to be high. Figure 7.3 shows a parking area in the Borough of Hackney, London. This is an initiative between *Ofo* (a large Chinese dockless bike share firm) and a commercial bike parking infrastructure company (Cyclehoop), as well as the Borough itself. These organisations have worked together to produce designated dockless bike share parking. These areas replace a car parking bay and can be very prominent, using the bright Ofo yellow. The Ofo App alerts users where these areas are and when users are required to park bikes in them. Basic information is also provided on how to download the App.

These spaces are free of any locking devices and simply serve as an easily recognisable area in which to park bikes in a way that minimise public nuisance issues that are inevitable with randomly parked bicycles.

In quieter residential areas, it is not necessary to designate corrals, but additional hoop parking should be provided to highlight areas suitable for dockless bicycle parking. It is often the case in North America that dockless bikes are able to park at bicycle parking hoops installed for private bikes, as cities know that these areas are in suitable locations for bike storage. If this leads to frustration from private cyclists, installing a greater number of hoops will benefit all users. This is the direction taken by many North American cities with dockless bike share.

The development of bicycle parking corrals, in conjunction with geofencing and other App-based measures to encourage the use of corrals, has been the most common effective response to reducing the parking issues associated with dockless bike share. Geofencing can be thought of as a 'digital fence' that works to encourage users to keep bicycles either *within*, or *outside* certain zones. For instance, if it has been decided that bicycle should not be parked directly outside the entrance to a large stadium, this area can be geofenced so that users are notified if they do try and end their trip in this area. Geofencing can also be used to highlight areas that are preferred parking zones. The App can direct people to these zones, to encourage their use and limit the number of bicycles randomly.

The development of permit application systems that outline the responsibilities for prospective dockless bike share operators seeking to set up in the city has also clarified the obligations they must meet. In some cases, this has included a fee, payable to the city authority. San Francisco requires any operator to fund the procurement and installation of one bicycle parking rack for every two bikes in their fleet.

Local governments will usually be best placed to identify the most appropriate areas to install these bicycle parking corrals. Local government should provide operators with geospatial files indicating the parts of their city where dockless bike share users are required to park. The operators would then be required to integrate this information into their App, informing bike share users of their need to park within these corrals when in activity areas or other high demand zones.

Finally, the degree to which the public and the media view dockless bike share as a *public nuisance* rather than *public service* is very much related to how much it is used. In some cities, it can be common for dockless bikes to sit idle for days, or even weeks, without attracting any riders. This serves to reinforce a public perception that these bicycles are a public nuisance, not serving a public need. Figure 7.4 offers a conceptual model illustrating the relationship between public acceptance and usage. As usage rises, so too does public acceptance (because the value to the community is evident). This model was developed after the author observed that the cities with well-used dockless bike share programs do not appear to attract the level of public criticism of low-usage programs.

The implication of this relationship for cities with dockless bike share, or planning to implement it, is that everything must be done to maximise its use. Whilst an effective agreement with bike share providers is critical, cities themselves need to ensure their bicycle infrastructure network, which encourages cycling. In most cases, this will mean substantial investments in protected bicycle lanes, off-road cycling connections and measures that boost the competitive advantage of bike share over private car use for short to medium distance inner city journeys. More information on how this can be achieved is provided in Chapters 9 and 10.

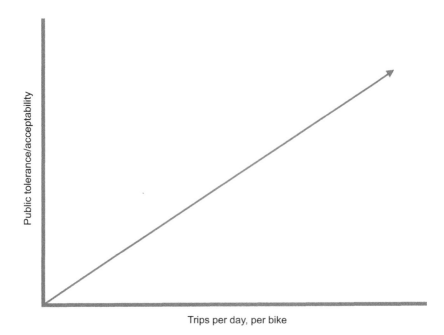

Figure 7.4 Relationship between public acceptance and usage: a conceptual model.
Source: Institute for Sensible Transport.

Notes

1 https://www.seattle.gov/transportation/docs/BicycleSharePermitRequirements.pdf
2 https://www.sfmta.com/sites/default/files/projects/2017/Bike%20Share%20Permit_v1.1_FINAL.pdf
3 http://content.tfl.gov.uk/dockless-bike-share-code-of-practice-september-2017.pdf
4 http://www.melbourne.vic.gov.au/news-and-media/Documents/Memorandum%20of%20Understanding%20-%20Extract%20of%20Roles%20and%20Responsibilities.pdf
5 https://www.cityofsydney.nsw.gov.au/explore/getting-around/cycling/dockless-bike-sharing

References

Fishman, E. (2017). *Bike Share Parking Infrastructure Guidelines.* Melbourne: Prepared by the Institute for Sensible Transport for VicRoads.
Institute for Transportation & Development Policy. (2018). The Bikeshare Planning Guide. Retrieved from New York: https://www.itdp.org/publication/the-bike-share-planning-guide/
Yanocha, D. (2018). Optimizing Dockless Bikeshare and Other Private New Mobility Services. Retrieved from New York: https://www.itf-oecd.org/optimising-dockless-bikeshare-and-other-private-new-mobility-services

8   The Business of Bike Share

Few sectors have experienced the rapid growth that bike share has over the last few years. New bike share firms, such as Mobike, which began in 2014 was purchased by Meituan Dianping for almost $US3 billion in 2018 (Russell, 2018). Many other new entrants to the bike share market have seen an influx of funding from outside firms. This is not restricted to the new, dockless bike share sector. More established firms, such as Motivate, have recently been purchased by Lyft, and seen an injection of funds to accelerate their expansion.

Companies specialise in a wide range of products and services to support the growth of bike share programs, from specialist bicycle suppliers, the technology that supports their use, or the hardware that make up docking stations and payment kiosks. Whilst some of these suppliers also operate bike share services (repair, maintenance, bike redistribution and call centre), there are also firms that focus solely on the operational responsibilities associated with bike share. A small number of firms also work to find large corporate sponsorship to allow bike share to be delivered at the lowest direct cost to the tax payer. A simplified conceptual framework of the architecture describing the bike share industry is shown in Figure 8.1.

It should be noted that whilst Figure 8.1 encapsulates the typical framework between the different elements of the bike share business model, this appears to be changing with the emergence of dockless bike share providers. Under a 'typical' dockless bike share model, the commercial operator/ supplier interacts directly with the end user (rider), with minimal, if any, interaction with the other parties listed in Figure 8.1. As described in Chapter 7, there has been a tendency from some dockless bike share companies to enter markets without negotiation or consultation with government. This is now beginning to change, with some companies recognising that unlike car-based ride sources services like Uber, dockless bike share requires designated places to park bikes as a fundamental element of its business model.

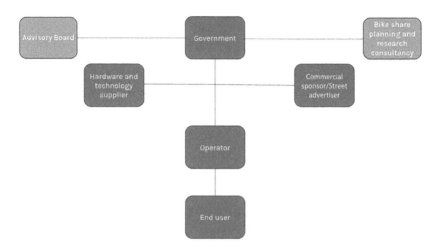

Figure 8.1 The business of bike share: a conceptual model. Source: Elliot Fishman, Institute for Sensible Transport.

8.1 Operational Structures

A diverse range of business models have emerged to support the global growth of bike share. Street advertising was one popular mode of bike share provision that was prominent during the 2005–2013 period. In this model, street advertising contracts were used to partially or fully fund docked bike share services (e.g., Paris). This has become less common, as dockless bike has begun offering services at zero or no direct cost to government. Some prominent programs still rely on sponsorship arrangements, such as the Citi Bike program in New York and the Ford GoBike system in San Francisco.

The variety of models currently employed to plan, deliver and operate bike share are introduced in this chapter. These range from fully publicly owned, to entirely commercial programs. The model of delivery is probably not quite as important as the contract that determines the degree to which incentives are in place to maximise bike share use.

1   **Government owned, with private-sector operator.** *Capital Bikeshare* in Washington, D.C. and *Melbourne Bike Share* employ this model, with Government owning and financing the program, which is then operated by a private-sector operator. The private-sector operator often subcontracts a smaller bike share operations firm to manage the bikes (e.g., servicing, replacement and re-distribution). Some of the docked Chinese bike share systems are run as public private partnerships, although this model has not been as effective as fully government run in terms of ridership (Lohry & Yiu, 2015).

2   **Government owned and operated.** This model replicates the manner in which most city rail agencies are structured, whereby the government own the hardware and operating system and are responsible for all day-to-day and strategic requirements. Whilst there are no North American examples of this model known to the author, it is commonplace in China for docked systems (Lohry & Yiu, 2015), often with no or very little direct cost to the rider.

3   **Non-Government Organisation (NGO) owned.** This model is common in North America and involves an NGO being formed (or pre-existing) to own the system, and either manages and operates the bike share program itself, or contracts this out to a bike share operator. Funding is primarily from government, with additional revenue streams through commercial sponsorship and rider fees/charges. The responsibility for all day-to-day activities associated with running the bike share program usually reside with the contractor operator, and the NGO takes administrative responsibilities for non-day-to-day tasks. A Board of Directors is usually formed to make strategic decisions and can be composed of private-sector sponsors, government representatives and suitably qualified members of the community.

4   **Commercially owned and operated.** *Citi Bike* in New York City employ this model, as do the newly established San Francisco bike share program, known as *Ford Gobike*. The commercial operator is typically responsible for securing a sponsor/fundraising and also relies on rider fees as a form of revenue generation to help cover costs. The government has less control over system design and expansion, as well as access to data, unless written into the contract. Whilst reliance on public funds is lessened in this model, it is not uncommon for government to subsidise the system, either with direct funding, or through in kind support. For *CityCycle* in Brisbane, Australia as well as many of the bike share programs in Europe, a street advertiser, such as JC Decaux acts as the commercial owner and operator, in return for outdoor advertising contracts, often with a life of one or two decades (20 years in Brisbane's case). Some scholars have raised concerns that by designing bike share to be reliant on commercial sponsorship, this may influence the degree to which the bike share provider will be willing to extend their service to less affluent part of this city (Duarte, 2016), with obvious equity concerns.

Box 8.1 Two bike share businesses

JC Decaux

The French street advertising firm JC Decaux revolutionised bike share by integrating it with street advertising contracts. This lowered the financial outlay city authorities were required to pay in

(Continued)

upfront costs, making it more palatable, from a budgetary perspective. JC Decaux, which paid the US$115 million establishment cost for the Velib system in Paris (Duarte, 2016), became prominently involved in bike share, and this was largely due to the pivotal role it played in the first 10 years of the Velib system, which is now run by another operator, *Smoove*. As JC Decaux's flagship program, Velib, with over 20,000 bicycles and between 120,000 and 140,000 trips per day in summer popularised global bike share. With over 300,000 annual subscribers (12% of the Paris population), JC Decaux reports that 40% of all bike trips in the Paris capital are now done using their *Velib* bikes. The system generates between €16 and €18 million in annual user fee revenue and under JC Decaux's contract with the City of Paris, this is all returned to the local government. This is somewhat unique to Paris, and in cities not able to generate the advertising revenue of Paris, other revenue sharing arrangements are in place.

JC Decaux has not attracted any large cities to its bike share model for over 8 years. The last city to install a JC Decaux bike share system of more than 1,000 bikes was Brisbane, Australia, in 2010. As described in Chapter 9, one of the complexities of a street advertiser-run bike share program is that the incentive to maximise ridership is not always clear, and policies can be put in place that thwart rather than encourage ridership. For instance, in Brisbane, when bike share was initially launched, the system closed between 10 pm and 5 am, and no credit card swipe option was offered at the docking stations.

Motivate

Motivate is the largest bike share company in North America and previously started as an offshoot of the Portland, Oregon-based consultancy *Alta Planning*. A name change from *Alta Bike Share* to *Motivate* took place in 2014, following its acquisition by Bikeshare Holdings LLC. In 2018, Motivate was acquired by Lyft, the App-based ride sourcing service.

Motivate works with city authorities to deliver bike share programs, often through financial arrangements with corporate brands. For instance, its flagship program, *Citi Bike* in New York was delivered via corporate sponsorship with *Citi Bank* and *MasterCard*, who contributed $US46m and $US5m, respectively, for a multi-year sponsorship deal. Similarly, in San Francisco, Motivate was able to secure the car manufacturer Ford as the naming rights sponsor, in return for ~$US47 million over 7 years. In the case of New York

City and San Francisco, the basic promise within the *Motivate* pitch is that it can deliver programs at no or minimal public expense. As a company, it takes the risk that sponsorship and revenue from ridership will be larger than what it cost to provide the system. It owns the system but shares user revenue with the city. In other cities, such as Portland, Motivate operates the BIKETOWN bike share program with some funds coming from the city to meet the capital costs of establishing the system (e.g., bikes and other infrastructure). In other Motivate-run bike share programs (such as Washington, D.C.), it holds a contract to operate the system for a fee, and the system is owned by the government jurisdictions covering the bike share area.

Source: Albert Asseraf (JC Decaux) provided information during an interview with the author (Asseraf, 2016). Jay Walder, CEO of Motivate, provided written responses to the author's questions. These responses were used to develop the material in the above box.

Of the typologies of bike share business models identified above, examples of system success and failure can be found in each. As identified earlier in this chapter, it is vital that city governments build *incentives* into their contracts with private bike share providers, to ensure that usage is maximised. Without these incentives, it is plausible that companies deriving income from non–bike share sources (e.g., street advertising), might leave the bike share service to languish, as the operational cost savings this provides is greater than the revenue they think is achievable from running the bike share service properly.

Incentivisation to maximise use is the most pertinent structural[1] determinant of bike share performance. Should a contract be signed with a bike share provider/operator in which no commercial benefit is offered by increasing usage levels, it may indeed become *more* profitable for the operator to *constrain* usage, by reducing opening hours, preventing instantaneous membership via automated credit card swipe, etc.

8.2 Contract Considerations

Contracts that provide sufficient commercial incentives to maximise program use will enjoy higher usage levels, greater customer satisfaction and higher return on investment for government. This return on investment also includes maximising the key benefits of bike share discussed in Chapter 4. Incentivisation is usually operationalised via a revenue sharing arrangement in which the operator stands to financially gain for higher usage levels.

The two key contract types involved in bike share relate to the supply of hardware (e.g., bikes, docking stations, supporting technology) and operations (e.g., call centre, bike repair and redistribution). Given the diversity and increasing maturity of the bike share industry, it can be wise to be open to the possibility of separate contracts with each of these providers, as this could offer a better platform for competition and provide a greater level of protection should one supplier go bankrupt. On the other hand, one supplier for both the hardware and operations may offer a seamless, integrated organisational structure for program delivery, reducing the potential conflict or blame shifting from having two separate suppliers.

A contract must contain clearly articulated, measurable standards regarding bicycle repair and maintenance, monitoring method and penalties for failure to meet these standards (Fishman, Schmitt, & Baker, 2016). The contract should seek to minimise risk to government entities and place this risk onto the hardware provider and the operator. Punitive fines should be clearly outlined when minimum standards have not been met and should avoid the possibility that government will be required to commit additional funds that were not explicitly agreed to in the contractual phase. Contracts should outline the responsibilities of the bike share supplier for a number of areas and include a number of Key Performance Indicators (KPIs) with incentives to satisfactorily meet KPIs. Wherever possible, KPIs should be SMART – that is, Specific, Measurable, Attainable, Relevant and Timely. Stipulations should be included in case service levels or other KPIs are not met. Deductions, or revenue penalties, should be included in contracts for service failures (Fishman et al., 2016).

In some cases, it may be beneficial to ask respondents to Request for Proposals (RFP) to detail their proposed approach to certain design elements, rather than dictating all of these within the RFP. This is especially important now that the commercial bike share sector has increased its level of innovation and creativity. Government should seek to encourage rather than restrict the creative, competitive forces that are currently present in the bike share industry. The emergence of dockless bike share provides a new opportunity for government to efficiently secure a bike share operator at vastly lower cost than many of the docked bike share systems. A good example can be seen from the Gold Coast, in eastern Australia. As the site for the 2018 Commonwealth Games, Gold Coast City Council were keen to establish bike share and put out a RFP. They selected the large Chinese firm Mobike, who supplied 2,000 bicycles (some with surfboard carry racks), and under the terms of the agreement, Mobike will be the only bike share firm able to operate in the city (Fishman, 2017). Using an RFP method, cities are able to dictate the terms under which a dockless bike share firm enters their city, to help ensure it delivers the outcomes important to them.

Other considerations when beginning to develop contracts between government and commercial bike share suppliers include (Fishman et al., 2016):

- Contract duration (e.g., initial term duration – 10 years) with potential for further extensions and incentives to upgrade hardware/technology on a regular basis.
- Bike share data to be provided in open, standardised format and include a 'dashboard' interface on a publicly available website.
- Information collected in a format that allows for easy analysis of trends and opportunities for expansion and optimisation of the program (including collecting data in multiple choice or drop-down menus rather than solely open text).

Finally, it is important for the government agencies planning bike share to be aware that many bike share operators work in dozens of cities and this provides them with the skills and experience to make shrewd decisions that are in their commercial interest and potentially to the detriment of the government/public. Recognising this, government must conduct careful due diligence prior to entering into a contract for the supply and operation of a bike share program. This may require the involvement of a specialist bike share advisor, who can help to balance the knowledge discrepancy that often exists between government and commercial bike share providers. Speaking with city officials in other jurisdictions may also provide insights useful in making a decision regarding the preferred provider.

8.3 Bike Share Costs

What does it cost to establish and run a bike share program? Understandably, this is often the first question a city government will ask when beginning to consider a bike share program. Unfortunately, there is no easy answer, and it can range from almost nothing to up to $US11,000 or more per bike. Public funds can be minimised by choosing a dockless firm, who, at least in 2018, are prepared to enter a city without public subsidy. Whilst there is no guarantee this will continue, there is currently no lack of enthusiasm for this business model, although in cities without strong characteristics for bike use, it can be difficult to understand how their model generates a healthy profit. For cities like New York and San Francisco, the appeal from advertisers means that the revenue from sponsorship of docked bike share can largely meet the cost of providing the system, once user revenue is also included.

Ultimately, it will be the type of bike, whether it is docked or dockless, whether it has electric assist and the size of the system that will determine cost. Another important factor is the type of business model through which the bike share system might be delivered. Does it make sense for the city to opt for a street advertising/sponsorship provided contract or are other mechanisms favoured for the delivery of a bike share program? Often, a city may have specific regulatory codes that restrict opportunities for street advertising. These must be considered before selecting the most suitable bike share business model.

This section is intended to provide some general indications of cost associated with the establishment and operation of an urban bike share program. It is focused primarily on docked systems rather than dockless models, because in the majority of cases, the dockless systems do not require a price list, as they are typically offered without direct cost to cities.

For cities considering the introduction of a bike share program, arriving at a reasonably firm cost estimate can be difficult, even if there is an understanding about the type and size of bike share program required. This is because it is typical for commercial providers to withhold detailed costs until submitting a formal response to *Requests for Quotation*. Nevertheless, it is possible, using publicly available data and direct communication with hardware suppliers to provide some cost estimates. Whilst every effort has been taken to ensure the accuracy of the figures included in this section, they are likely to fluctuate over time and will increase for those cities categorised as 'remote' (i.e., a considerable distance from the supplier's main market). This can have implications for southern hemisphere cities in particular.

In broad terms, the cost of providing a bike share system can be separated into *Capital Expenditure* and *Operating Expenditure*, in addition to pre-launch planning and marketing activities. These costs are described below.

8.3.1 Capital Expenditure Estimates

Bike share capital expenditure consists primarily of the bikes themselves and their associated docking infrastructure and payment kiosks. Dockless systems do of course avoid the need to purchase and install docking infrastructure, making their establishment faster and cheaper.

For docked bike share systems (such as *Citi Bike* in New York or *Velib* in Paris), the industry standard is to provide a ratio of two docking points for each bicycle (Institute for Transportation & Development Policy, 2013). It is difficult to compare the prices from different suppliers, as some include their technological components within the docking station (the so-called 'smart dock, dumb bike' model that was described in Section 6.1), whereas other providers include the technology within the bicycles themselves, described as 'dumb dock, smart bike,' in Section 6.2.

The costs for a docked, electric assist bike share service, including the docking infrastructure and the bicycles, range from between $US6,000 and $US11,000 per bike. When investigating bike share suppliers, it is recommended government agencies exercise the competitive forces of the market by developing a *RFP* document that identifies the minimum requirements and allows commercial suppliers to submit their proposals. The commercial bike share sector has never been more competitive, with a growing number of new entrants to the market and innovative technology that promises to enhance the functionality of the system and user experience. Non-competitive arrangements with a single supplier should be avoided, if not already prohibited by existing procurement regulations. Allowing the dynamics of the current marketplace to compete for the contract to supply and operate a bike share system will be of benefit to the city agency, tax payer and end user.

8.3.2 Pre-launch Start-Up Costs

Preparatory activities required to plan a bike share program are not insubstantial. New York City, for instance, required at least 4 years of planning prior to the launch of the successful *Citi Bike* program. The initial phase, which can begin after the completion of a feasibility study and the subsequent development of a *Request for Quotation* (RFQ) document, is likely to include a number of investments, including the following:

- Staff salaries
- Office
- IT services and website development
- Community consultation
- Market research, branding and graphic design development
- Sponsorship search and negotiation
- Insurance and legal costs
- Technical design of catchment location and docking station siting.

Figure 8.2 is taken from the bike share feasibility study for Adelaide, Australia (Fishman, 2016a). Many of the tasks identified in Figure 8.2 will be relevant for cities without a strong bicycling culture or infrastructure. The development of a network of protected bicycle lanes and paths is considered a critical element of bike share success, as demonstrated in a recent meta-analysis of 75 different bike share programs (Médard de Chardon, Caruso, & Thomas, 2017). The bike share programs in Brisbane and Melbourne offer pertinent examples of what happens when cities implement bike share *before* the necessary supportive infrastructure has been built, with both programs struggling to attract riders (Atfield, 2016; Fishman, 2015; Fishman, Washington, Haworth, & Mazzei, 2014). One item included in Figure 8.2 is the examination of a *helmet waiver*, which of course only applies to the handful of cities that mandate the wearing of helmets for adults riding bicycles. Mandatory helmet legislation has been

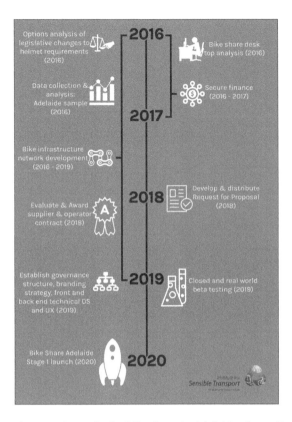

Figure 8.2 Implementation tasks for bike share in Adelaide, Australia.
Source: Fishman (2016a).

a contentious issue in jurisdictions to which it applies and has been magnified by the introduction of bike share. A discussion of the relationship between bike share and the requirement for a blanket helmet requirement is offered in Section 9.7.

The time periods in Figure 8.2 may appear rather long to some readers. This is due to the magnitude of some of the tasks required to be undertaken. The development of enhanced bicycle infrastructure is rarely a rapid process. Moreover, the completion of complex studies regarding the total population health impact of a waiver to mandatory helmet laws is unlikely to be completed within a short time frame. Under special circumstances, in which a concerted effort is made with sufficient resources, it may be possible to streamline this process, bringing it down to two to three years. Of course for cities without mandatory helmet laws for adults, and with a comprehensive network of separated bicycle routes, planning and implementing a bike share system can be completed more rapidly.

8.3.3 Operational Expenditure Estimates

The costs involved in operating and maintaining a bike share program are significant. It is typical for a docked bike share system to incur per bike, annual costs of around $US2,000. Whilst this may be modest compared to conventional public transport systems (e.g., trains, light rail, buses), many people would be initially surprised at the cost of maintaining a bike share system.

Typically, a government will enter into a contract with a bike share operations firm, who will charge a $/dock rate. For instance, in 2016, Arlington (government entity) pay Motivate (bike share operator) $US96.17/dock/month. This covers the cost of fleet redistribution, servicing and replacement of bike hardware, as well as customer service/call centre costs and costs associated with maintaining software, a website and mobile App. For some systems, there are also software licencing fees, which are generally monthly payments to connect the bicycles to the 'cloud', enabling GPS tracking and other remote features. These software fees can be higher for the smart bike (dockless) model of bike share, as each bicycle may require a connection to the cloud. Redistribution of bicycles accounts for the majority of operational expenditure in many docked bike share programs. Box 8.2 provides an overview of redistribution.

Box 8.2 Rebalancing bike share systems

Rebalancing refers to bike share operators moving bicycles across the network, to maintain a reasonable distribution across docking stations (Fishman, Washington, & Haworth, 2014). The need for rebalancing is caused when 'tidal flows' of bike share trips move from or to certain areas of a city, such as from residential to commercial zones in morning peak hour. This leads to some stations being completely full whilst others are empty. This can result in a lack of reliability for the user and reduced satisfaction (Transport for London, 2014), as well as significant costs imposed on operators to manually redistribute the fleet, to maintain a reasonable distribution across docking stations (Fishman, Washington, & Haworth, 2014).

These twin issues have spurred a diverse range of investigations into effective measures to improve fleet redistribution. Most bike redistribution takes place through the use of trucks and vans. The below image shows a truck involved in rebalancing activities in one of Europe's most used bike share programs, *Bicing* in Barcelona. Operators attempt to conduct redistribution activities in the off-peak period; however, there are times when this is not possible, as peak

---

(Continued)

demand for bike share is generally the same as for general traffic. *Citi Bike* in New York City as well as bike share programs in other cities have employed specially fitted trailers powered by electric assist bicycles to enable redistribution in heavy traffic. These trailers can generally carry up to 12 bicycles at a time. A number of big city systems also provide a 'valet service' in which a staff member can accept bicycles in areas designated to take docking station overflow for sites that routinely exceed capacity.

Bike share programs in hilly cities can experience major redistribution problems, given the general reluctance to ride a heavy bike share bike up hill. Paris experienced this problem soon after the launch of the *Velib* system in 2007. Since then, a common response to this issue has been to avoid placing docking stations in hilly parts of the city. This was the approach taken in San Francisco and Brisbane. The emergence of e-bike share would appear to offer an effective solution for hilly cities looking to avoid the issue of topography contributing to rebalancing problems. This is part of the reason a portion of the new bikes delivered as part of the Velib system in Paris will offer electric assistance.

The possibility of 'gamification' and other incentives to enable bike share riders themselves to contribute to rebalancing has not yet received widespread adoption. A number of operators are exploring whether the smartphone may be able to act as a platform for providing 'nudges' to users on 'reverse flow' movements, and when a rider performs such a movement, receive a reward (e.g., extra week of membership). In lieu of such a system, technology may enable bicycles to lock to themselves where a docking station has reached capacity. One of the more prominent examples of having users re-balance bicycles is Citi Bike's *Bike Angels* program, such is described in the following section.

8.3.4 Gamifying the Re-balancing Task: Citi Bike's Bike Angels Program

Given the costly logistical challenge of re-balancing already identified in this chapter, bike share operators clearly have a financial incentive in minimising staff time involved in re-distributing bikes across the network. In New York, Citi Bike has 120 staff dedicated to the re-balancing task. In an effort to lower the cost associated with this task, an incentive-based rebalancing program called *Bike Angels* was introduced. The program offers points to Citi Bike users to either rent a bike from a full station or return a bike to a low-occupancy station. *Bike Angels* earn monthly, annual, and lifetime points with additional rewards available throughout the year. As of April 2017, there are over 30,000 registered Bike Angels. Reports suggest that Bike Angels account for more than 40% of rebalancing on busy days.

Points are determined by the current fill level and the future flow of bikes. The score map is updated every 16 minutes. Bike Angels can earn up to five points per trip if special promotions are running, though most are between 1 and 3 points. Measures are put in place to prevent Bike Angels from 'gaming' the system (e.g., biking back and forth between two stations). Angels caught gaming the system will have those points removed.

Monthly Rewards
- 10 points: One 24-hour day pass
- 20–80 points: Free 1-week membership extension for every 20 points
- 80+ points: Gift cards $1 per 10 points above 80

Annual Rewards
- 250 points: Rapid rentals (removal of 2-minute wait time between rentals)
- 500 points: Bike share passes for Divvy (Chicago), Blue Bikes (Boston), Ford GoBike (San Francisco)

Lifetime Rewards
- 250 points: Engraved pin
- 500 points: White Citi Bike key
- 1,500 points: Bike Angels water bottle and tote bag
- 2,500 points: Steel Angel Key

Two types of Bike Angels have emerged from the program: regular users and 'Power Angels' (Parker, 2017). Regular users are defined as people who use *Citi Bike* regularly and picking up some points occasionally to discount their membership fee. *Power Angels* are high-earning Citi Bike users, taking part in the program to accumulate maximum points. Citi Bike offers several additional promotions for Power Angels, including a monthly leader board listing the top 10 Angels. Cash prizes are available for the top 5 Angels each month. Record holders are also displayed on the Citi Bike website for maximum daily, monthly and yearly points.

As of July 2018, *Capital Bikeshare* in Washington, D.C. has introduced a similar scheme. In May, San Francisco's *Ford GoBike* began a Bike Angels program.

8.4 Bike Share Revenue

Bike share revenue is generated from two key sources: (1) commercial sponsorship and (2) user fees/charges.

8.4.1 Commercial Sponsorship

As highlighted earlier, commercial sponsorship plays an important role in many bike share programs (Duarte, 2016). The sponsorship of bike share brings increased brand awareness to the sponsoring company and may also assist those firms seeking to develop a reputation for sustainable practices and innovation. Revenue from a commercial sponsor is generally expected to be a function of the size of the potential market an advertiser's product or service is exposed to. For instance, New York City's bike share program, *Citi Bike* enjoys high levels of public exposure, owing to the size and profile of the city. This has allowed *Citi Bike* to attract $US41 million over 5 years from *Citibank*, as well as an additional $US6 million from *MasterCard*. Table 8.1 provides an indication from a selected number of bike share programs for which commercial sponsorship data are available.

Table 8.1 Bike share programs with a principal commercial sponsor

City	Program	Operator	Principal sponsor/s	Annual amount
London	Santander Cycles	Serco	Santander	£6.4 million
New York City	Citi Bike	Motivate	Citi and MasterCard	US$41 million + US$6 million
San Francisco	FordGoBike	Motivate	Ford	US$7 million
Minneapolis/ St. Paul	NiceRide	NiceRide Minnesota	Blue Cross and Blue Shield of Minnesota	US$750,000 + US$200,000 for non-principal sponsor
Portland	BikeTown	Motivate	Nike	US$2 million
Barcelona	Bicing	ClearChannel	Vodafone	€1.45 million

Box 8.3 Ford's Sponsorship of Bay Area Bike Share

Whilst it is difficult to estimate the *return on investment* for the corporate sponsorship of bike share, it is illustrative to look briefly at the sponsorship of the Ford Motor Company's title sponsorship of the recently launched Bay Area bike share program. The automobile industry is currently in a state of flux, with Uber and other ride sourcing services making it easier for the public to envision a future in which they use cars as a *service* to be accessed, rather than a good to be owned. This, coupled with the emergence of autonomous vehicles presents a major disruptive force to established motor vehicle manufacturers like Ford. The entry of technology companies into the mobility industry (e.g., Google's Waymo, Apple) is an additional reason why automobile manufacturers are seeking to *reinvent* themselves as 'mobility service companies'. By securing the sponsorship of the Bay Area bike share program, Ford is able to project a corporate image that says it understands and embraces a future in which car ownership is no longer the default method urban dwellers gain access to mobility. Jessica Robinson, Director of *Ford City Solutions*, has said that whilst it has no plans to stop selling cars, the business model it has used for over 100 years 'can't continue' (Peters, 2017). Ford's entry into bike share is one of a number of investments it is making into transport innovation in which the widespread need for individual car ownership becomes a thing of the past. Ford intends to use its involvement in bike share to gain insights into the user experience and mobility patterns in an attempt to remain relevant in the rapidly evolving urban transport landscape.

Once government have developed the detailed program design features for their bike share program (e.g., indicative size of the catchment, number and type of bikes), it may be necessary to develop a *prospectus*, if it feels their city is in a position to attract commercial sponsorship. The prospectus and associated website will allow prospective commercial and government sponsors to assess the benefits of involvement and levels of contribution, from naming rights sponsor, through to the sponsoring of individual docking stations. Increasingly, it would appear that the process of securing a naming rights sponsor is undertaken by a third party rather than directly by government.

The most appropriate naming rights/principal sponsor is likely to be one with a particular affiliation with the city, and a connection with at least one of the elements bike share relates to (e.g., sustainability, health, fun, transport, cost-effectiveness, convenience, sharing economy). Some examples are provided below (not exhaustive):

- *Department of Health or Health Insurer:* Health is the largest beneficiary from increased population levels of cycling (Mulley, Tyson, McCue, Rissel, & Munro, 2013), and bike riding is recognised as an effective preventative behaviour reducing sedentary lifestyle disease (Fishman, Böcker, & Helbich, 2015; Fishman, Schepers, & Kamphuis, 2015; Fishman, Washington, & Haworth, 2015). The relationship between cycling and healthy living makes for a potentially strong partnership between health departments/insurer and bike share. Many corporate sponsors of bike share in North America are healthcare/health insurance companies.

- *Technology sector*: Bike share systems are increasingly adopting innovative technologies to manage the customer interface and operational logistics of bike share (e.g., Near Field Communication, GPS, QR Codes). Technology companies may see a synergy between bike share and their desire to be viewed as a progressive, urban solution that enhances a city's productivity.
- *Finance/banking*: A number of large bike share programs have the banking sector as their principal sponsor. The initial London bike share program, *Barclays Cycle Hire*, and the current NYC bike share program *Citi Bike* are two prominent examples. It would appear that this sector, which spends considerable capital on marketing, has an appetite for building an association with bike share.
- *Sharing economy:* The growth of so-called 'sharing economy' platforms (e.g., AirBnB, Turo, SnappCar) offers a synergistic relationship with bike share and may help to increase marketplace awareness. The growth projections for the sharing economy suggest that these platforms may be able to inject much needed capital into newly established bike share programs. Car share, *Uber* and *AirBnB* are some of the major platforms that might see a benefit in the exposure gained by sponsorship of a bike share program.
- *Electricity supplier*: There is an obvious (and currently untapped) synergy between a major electricity company, and a bike share program that offers electric assist bicycles. For energy retailers in deregulated energy markets, the opportunity to sponsor a bike share program would appear compelling, especially if the retailer has a desire to promote renewable energy, given the strong link between cycling and sustainability (Banister, 2005; Fishman, 2016b; Hickman & Banister, 2014).

The above offers an initial selection of the type of companies and sectors that may have an interest in aligning with a future bike share program. This list is by no means exhaustive, and there would appear to be a trend for sectors without any direct affinity with cycling to sponsor bike share programs. Examples include financial institutions (e.g., London's Santander Cycle Hire, previously Barclays Cycle Hire), and more recently motor vehicle manufacturers, as previously identified.

8.4.2 User Fees

Although there is some minor variability, almost all modern, docked bike share programs (third-generation bike share) broadly have the same general fee structure. This includes a choice of membership, or 'subscription' periods (e.g., annual, monthly, daily), with additional usage fees only charged for trips in excess of 30 minutes. Some systems have a 45-minute period before additional usage fees are incurred. The general experience among systems globally is that around 90–95% of trips are completed within the

Table 8.2 Bike share subscription rates, selected cities

City	Casual			Registered	
	Single trip	1 day	3 day	30 day	Annual
Washington, D.C.	$2	$8	–	–	$85
Montreal	$C2.95	$C5	$C14	$C32	$C91
London		£2	–	–	£90
San Francisco	$2	$10	–	$15	$149
Boston	$2.50	$10[a]	$15	–	$99
Minneapolis/St. Paul	$2	$6	–	–	$75
NYC	$3	$12	$24	–	$169[b]
Chicago	$3	$15	–	–	$99/75[c]
Melbourne[d]		$A3	–		$A60
Brisbane[e]		$A2	–	$5/$3	–
Paris[f]	Free	€6	–	€8.30	€99.60/€39[g]

a An *Adventure Pass* offers unlimited access to 2-hour trips in a 24-hour period.
b NYC's Citi Bike offers annual subscribers 45 minutes before excess usage charges are incurred, per trip.
c The lower price is a student membership.
d Melbourne Bike Share offers annual subscribers 45 minutes before excess usage charges are incurred, per trip.
e Has weekly, three-monthly, and annual passes instead.
f Pricing refers to V-Max (e-bike) subscriptions. Single trip pricing for <30 minutes.
g These prices are for 30 minutes/45 minutes as the free period per trip. Paris offers a range of discounted prices for youth/students.
NB: Prices as of 23 December 2018.
NB: Some systems offer discount rates to students and age-related discounts. Some membership periods not listed here. All currency US Dollars unless shown otherwise.

'free' period, and this is especially true for trips by annual members, who are more price sensitive and less inclined to 'explore' the city (Fishman, 2014). Table 8.2 provides an outline of user costs for a selection of bike share programs.

The Chinese dockless bike share providers tend to operate a different pricing structure to those shown in Table 8.2. Typically, they offer a pay-per-trip pricing structure (e.g., 99 cents per 30 minutes). It would appear too early to know whether this model is viable. Dockless bike share sometimes offer a subscription model similar to that shown in *Table 8.2,* but it can often be less prominently advertised than their per trip price.

Membership revenue from the London bike share program is shown in Figure 8.3. This is shown as a percentage of total usage fees (not including charges imposed on those whose rental period is longer than 30 minutes). The total revenue generated from usage fees is £6.3 million, broken down as shown in Figure 8.3. These proportions are broadly similar to other bike share programs, with the general pattern being that daily access fees generate a substantially higher rate of return to operators, compared to the amount of riding they account for. Annual members contribute less, on a $/km basis than do casual users.

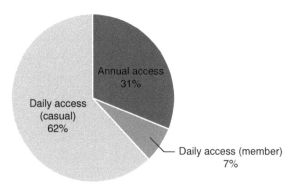

Figure 8.3 Usage fees from the London bike share program.
Source: Transport for London (2016).

It is important to recognise that the user fees generated from high-density cities with large-scale bike share programs (e.g., NYC, Barcelona, Paris and London) is unlikely to be replicable in smaller cities. Moreover, the high levels of tourists in the aforementioned cities also boosts revenue, over and above ridership levels because each tourist generally pays a higher fee because they tend to require casual rather than annual membership. Cities seeking to establish a bike share program must consider these factors when developing estimates of the revenue generated from user fees and chargers.

8.5 Summary of Costs and Revenue

The costs of establishing a bike share program include the hardware (bikes and docking stations), the software and technology platform, as well as network planning and marketing and management costs.

The operating costs of bike share include fleet redistribution, serving, repair and replacement, as well as customer service costs.

In most cases, bike share program operators are not obliged to disclose their capital and operating costs. In general, however, it is estimated that most modern, docked bike share programs have capital costs of around $US5,000–$US10,000 per bike, which include the supporting infrastructure such as docking stations, computer systems, control centre and maintenance and marketing expenditure.

Table 8.3 provides as detailed a breakdown as possible of the costs and revenue associated with several bike share programs. These figures should be taken as a guide, as each bike share operator may have different methods of calculating their costs and revenue. Of the many operators approached, only three (Washington, D.C., London and Minneapolis) provided sufficient information to report on their operating cost recovery

Table 8.3 Bike share costs and revenue

	Washington, D.C. Arlington only[a]	London	Dublin	Minneapolis
Number of bikes	600	11,095	1,500	1,704
Number of docking stations	81	775	100	190
Capital cost per bike	$1,231	Not public	N/A[b]	$1,313
Capital cost per docking spot	$1,660	Not public	N/A	$2,290
Annual operating cost per bike	$1,366	Not public	€1,280[c]	$997
Income from sponsorship (annual)	$50,000	£6,400,000	€300,000	$242,000
Income from user fees	$890,000	Not public		$1,200,269
Operating cost recovery[d]	63%	Not public	–	70.6%
Total cost recovery[e]	51%	–	–	–

Sources: Arlington's Capital Bike share (Washington, D.C.) provided to the author by Paul DeMaio. London's data provided by Transport for London. Dublin information provided by Michael Rossiter of Coca Cola dublinbikes, Mitch Vars provided Minneapolis data.
a Arlington only. Capital Bike share includes several jurisdictions and this data only includes the Arlington component. Financial Year 2015.
b The operator was not able to provide these costs; however, they do report that the recent system expansion of 950 bikes, and 57 stations cost €6.1 million.
c Estimate based on annual operating cost of $1.92 million.
d Operating cost recovery is the ratio of operating revenues divided by operating expenses (Arlington County, 2015).
e Total cost recovery is the ratio of operating revenues divided by the sum of operating, marketing and management expenses (Arlington County, 2015).
NB: All currency US Dollars unless shown otherwise.

ratio (operating revenues divided by operating expenses). In the case of London and Washington, D.C., they recover just over 60% of the costs incurred to operate their systems. Minneapolis achieved a cost recovery of just over 70%. Interestingly, these figures compare favourably with some conventional (motorised) public transport systems, especially from Australia and North America.

In summary, the costs associated with the establishment of a bike share program can be substantial but are modest when compared to other forms of public transport. The cost recovery ratio, where figures are provided, amounts to around 60% of operating costs. Usage fees vary only slightly between bike share programs and are generally designed to favour annual memberships and short trips under 30 minutes.

On a cautionary note, commercial bike share operators, many of which run dozens of systems as part of a global operation, often have more experience than government authorities in bike share contract preparation. This has previously led to instances in which the commercial provider/operator has achieved highly favourable contract terms, often resulting in reduced levels of service for potential users of the system. It is therefore imperative that government sources the necessary expertise to complement their staff's experience in contract management and transport policy. This will enable the crafting of *RFQ* documents that *build in* financial incentives linked to performance. Whilst this book does not provide an exhaustive review of other components a RFQ should include, the issue of *incentivisation* is considered paramount.

Finally, it is important to bear in mind that bike share is not generally able to meet its costs through revenue generated from user fees. Whilst there appears to be a trend towards governments stating an ambition to provide a *cost neutral* bike share program, this is highly contingent on the commercial attractiveness of the city (for prospective sponsorship arrangements) as well as projected revenue from user fees. In most cities, these two factors are unlikely to provide sufficient revenue to meet the establishment and operational costs of providing a bike share program. A good demonstration of this can be seen in the failed Melbourne attempt to have 'the market' offer cost neutral bike share when it sought to retender the contract in 2014. Melbourne received no compliant bids. There are no obvious reasons why a bike share program should be any more likely to run cost neutral than other elements of the public transport system (e.g., train, tram).

Note

1 Structural in this context pertains to the business structure through which bike share is delivered and operated.

References

Asseraf, A. (2016, 14th September) *JC Decaux and Bike Share/Interviewer: E. Fishman*.

Atfield, C. (2016). Mayor defends cost of Brisbane's CityCycle scheme. *Brisbane Times*. Retrieved from http://www.brisbanetimes.com.au/queensland/mayor-defends-cost-of-brisbanes-citycycle-scheme-20160607-gpdx6a.html

Banister, D. (2005). *Unsustainable Transport: City Transport in the New Century*. Abingdon: Routledge.

Duarte, F. (2016). Disassembling bike-sharing systems: Surveillance, advertising, and the social inequalities of a global technological assemblage. *Journal of Urban Technology, 23*(2), 103–115. doi:10.1080/10630732.2015.1102421

Fishman, E. (2014). *Bikeshare: Barriers, facilitators and impacts on car use* (PhD thesis by publication). Queensland University of Technology, Brisbane.

Fishman, E. (2015). Bikeshare: A review of recent literature. *Transport Reviews*, 1–22. doi:10.1080/01441647.2015.1033036

Fishman, E. (2016a). Bike Share Options for Adelaide. Retrieved from Melbourne: https://sensibletransport.org.au/wp-content/uploads/2016/02/Bike-share-Options-for-Adelaide-Stage-3-Report-1.04.16DB_LR.pdf

Fishman, E. (2016b). Cycling as transport. *Transport Reviews, 36*(1), 1–8. doi:10.1080/01441647.2015.1114271

Fishman, E. (2017). *Bike Share Parking Infrastructure Guidelines*. Melbourne: Prepared by the Institute for Sensible Transport for VicRoads.

Fishman, E., Böcker, L., & Helbich, M. (2015). Adult active transport in the Netherlands: An analysis of its contribution to physical activity requirements. *PloS ONE, 10*(4), e0121871. doi:10.1371/journal.pone.0121871

Fishman, E., Schepers, P., & Kamphuis, C. B. (2015). Dutch cycling: Quantifying the health and related economic benefits. *American Journal of Public Health*, e1–e3. doi:10.2105/AJPH.2015.302724

Fishman, E., Schmitt, L., & Baker, L. (2016). Sydney Bike Share Feasibility Study: Operational Recommendations. Retrieved from https://sensibletransport.org.au/project/sydney-bike-share-feasibility-study/

Fishman, E., Washington, S., & Haworth, N. (2014). Bike share's impact on car use: Evidence from the United States, Great Britain, and Australia. *Transportation Research Part D: Transport & Environment, 31*, 7. doi:10.1016/j.trd.2014.05.013

Fishman, E., Washington, S., & Haworth, N. (2015). Bikeshare's impact on active travel: Evidence from the United States, Great Britain, and Australia. *Journal of Transport & Health, 2*(2), 135–142. doi:10.1016/j.jth.2015.03.004

Fishman, E., Washington, S., Haworth, N., & Mazzei, A. (2014). Barriers to bikesharing: An analysis from Melbourne and Brisbane. *Journal of Transport Geography, 41*, 325–337.

Hickman, R., & Banister, D. (2014). *Transport, Climate Change and the City*. Abingdon: Routledge.

Institute for Transportation & Development Policy. (2013). The Bike-sharing Planning Guide. Retrieved from New York: https://www.itdp.org/the-bike-share-planning-guide-2/

Lohry, G. F., & Yiu, A. (2015). Bikeshare in China as a public service: Comparing government-run and public-private partnership operation models. *Natural Resources Forum, 39*(1), 41–52. doi:10.1111/1477–8947.12063

Médard de Chardon, C., Caruso, G., & Thomas, I. (2017). Bicycle sharing system 'success' determinants. *Transportation Research Part A: Policy and Practice, 100*, 202–214.

Mulley, C., Tyson, R., McCue, P., Rissel, C., & Munro, C. (2013). Valuing active travel: Including the health benefits of sustainable transport in transportation appraisal frameworks. *Research in Transportation Business and Management, 7*, 27–34.

Parker, I. (2017). Hacking the Citi Bike points system. *The New Yorker*. Retrieved from https://www.newyorker.com/magazine/2017/12/04/hacking-the-citi-bike-points-system

Peters, A. (2017). The Bay Area's Expanding Bike Share is Part of Ford's Transition from Cars to "Mobility". Retrieved from https://www.fastcompany.com/40435791/the-bay-areas-expanding-bike-share-is-part-of-fords-transition-from-cars-to-mobility

Russell, J. (2018). Chinese Bike-sharing Pioneer Mobike Sold to Ambitious Meituan Dianping for $2.7B. Retrieved from https://techcrunch.com/2018/04/03/chinese-bike-sharing-pioneer-mobike-sold-to-ambitious-meituan-dianping-for-2-7b/

Transport for London. (2014). Barclays Cycle Hire Customer Satisfaction and Usage Survey: Members Only. Retrieved from London: http://www.tfl.gov.uk/cdn/static/cms/documents/barclays-cycle-hire-css-and-usage-members-q3-2013s-14.pdf

9   When Bike Share Goes Wrong

Melbourne and Brisbane are Australia's second and third largest cities, with populations of 5 million and 2.3 million people, respectively.[1] Both cities launched bike share programs in 2010, each of which have been characterised as having disappointing usage levels (e.g., see Atfield, 2016b; Fishman, 2012; Fishman, Washington, Haworth, & Watson, 2015; Ward, 2011). Both systems typically have less than one trip per day per bike (Atfield, 2016a, 2016b; Fishman, 2015). This is low by international standards (Fishman, 2015) and the intention of this chapter is to offer a synthesis of the factors that contributed to this under-utilisation, in order to reduce the possibility of other cities experiencing similar problems.

Table 9.1 provides a summary of the key metrics for both the Melbourne and Brisbane bike share programs.

Australia is in a somewhat unique position as one of only a handful of countries with mandatory helmet laws, across all age groups and all riding contexts (Haworth, Schramm, King, & Steinhardt, 2010). This makes bike share more difficult as it reduces the spontaneity with which people are able to use bike share (Fishman, Washington, Haworth, & Mazzei, 2014; Médard de Chardon, Caruso, & Thomas, 2017). Whilst mandatory helmet requirements are often the first factor people point to when looking at the low usage levels of Australian bike share programs, it is unlikely they are the only attributable factor (Fishman, 2012). A discussion of this topic is offered in Section 9.7.

Table 9.1 Melbourne and Brisbane bike share – key metrics

	Melbourne	*Brisbane*
Number of bikes	550	1,868
Average no. of trips per day, per bike (2015)	0.8	0.5
Catchment area	20 km^2	18 km^2
No. of docking stations	50	150
Funding model	State Government	Advertising + City Council

9.1 Australian Bike Share in the Beginning

The development of the Melbourne and Brisbane bike share programs were both initiated by political figures, keen to assert their credentials in sustainable mobility. This was especially the case in Brisbane, after some very large road building commitments threated to cement their reputation as overly focused on car-based transport planning.

For a relatively small budget, both the Victorian Government in Melbourne and Brisbane City Council in Brisbane were able to deliver bike share programs in a very short time period (relative to most other public transport investments). In Melbourne, a very small system (500–550 bicycles for a population of over 4.5 million) was entirely funded by the State Government (A\$5 million for the first four years). Brisbane chose a different funding model, similar to Paris's Velib, in which JC Decaux (the street advertising company) provides the bicycles and docking stations and operates the system in return for a 20-year contract for billboard advertisements, as well as marketing material on the bicycles themselves. JC Decaux earns revenue from these advertisements and provides the bike share program in return. This appeared attractive to Brisbane City Council. The Council has, however, been required to inject their own funds into the scheme. Reports suggest \$A14.6 million has been provided by Brisbane City Council in the 5 years to 2015. The program has returned \$A6.3 million in revenue over the same time period (Atfield, 2016b).

When initially proposed by then Brisbane City Council Lord Mayor Campbell Newman, CityCycle was envisioned to be cost-neutral; however, the current Lord Mayor Graham Quirk has argued that CityCycle should be seen as a component of the public transport system (Atfield, 2016b), which also costs more to run then it raises in revenue. Mayor Quirk has claimed that it is the long-term ambition for CityCycle to run cost-neutral (Atfield, 2016b), although this would appear to be highly unlikely over the remaining years of the current contract (expiry date 2030), based on existing usage.

One distinctive factor in the development of the Melbourne and Brisbane bike share programs was the lack of consultation and planning. Unlike most North American bike share programs, there were no community outreach or stakeholder engagement sessions with the community regarding the possible design features to maximise the success of the bike share program. No consultation was offered to refine the type of bicycles offered, the placement of the docking stations, sign-up procedure or helmets. The following section elaborates on each of these issues, in an effort to assist other cities seeking to establish a bike share program.

9.2 Barriers to Bike Share in Australia

The lower than expected usage levels of Australia's two bike share programs have led to a number of investigations regarding the barriers to bike share. This section offers an overview of the results of this research. To begin, however, it is important to recognise that undertaking research on barriers to bike share is more difficult than understanding the motivations for using bike share, as to gain an understanding of the barriers, you need to speak with people that have, almost by definition, shown little interest in bike share. Gaining responses to a set of questions regarding bike share can therefore prove difficult. These difficulties notwithstanding, a number of studies have examined the reasons people choose not to join bike share in Melbourne and Brisbane.

Six months after the launch of Melbourne Bike Share (MBS), the operators of the system conducted a market research exercise, motivated in part by lower than expected usage (Alta Bike Share, 2011), which hovered at around 0.3–0.5 trips per day, per bike. The survey was completed online by self-selected Internet users, and in the field by people walking in close proximity to a docking station. Just less than 500 people were surveyed in each method, and 31% of respondents had used MBS. It is important to recognise that these survey methods limit the generalizability of the results, as the sample only includes people who have visited the MBS website or walked past specific docking stations and were willing to participate in the survey. Nevertheless, the survey revealed some interesting findings about the barriers to using the scheme, as illustrated in Figure 9.1. In the period immediately following the launch of the MBS program, little attempt had been made to offer helmets to prospective riders, and the impact of this is shown in Figure 9.1, with a lack of helmet availability being the highest rating barrier, followed by not wanting to wear a helmet.

One contrasting feature between the results shown in Figure 9.1 and subsequent studies is that safety concerns did not feature prominently. An explanation for this is not obvious, but it may be that respondents attention

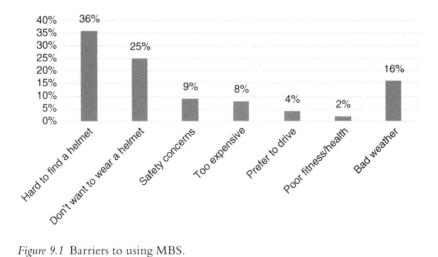

Figure 9.1 Barriers to using MBS.
Source: Alta Bike Share (2011).

was diverted by the perplexing situation of being presented with a bike share program without the necessary equipment to be able to legally use it. Some have likened this to a hire car company requiring their customers to bring their own seatbelt, a bowling alley asking customers to bring their own bowling shoes, or a bar expecting customers to bring their own glasses (Gutman, 2016).

Around 16% of respondents to the above survey identified 'bad weather' as a major barrier to bike share use. Whilst it might strike some people as unusual that an Australian bike share program would have 'bad weather' as a major barrier to usage, it is important to remember that beginning a bike share in May in the Southern Hemisphere (beginning of winter) reduces its appeal in the crucial first few months. As will be discussed further in Section 9.8, there are compelling reasons why a bike share program should not be launched in winter. In essence, it is important to launch at the time of year in which conditions are the most favourable, as the most effective bike share marketing is seeing someone else riding a shared bike. Getting as many positive determinants for bike share use in alignment, at the beginning of the program is critical to its long-term success.

In an effort to better understand the barriers to CityCycle in Brisbane, a survey was conducted with people who either lived, worked or were studying in Brisbane and had no known connection to bike share (Fishman et al., 2015). Of the 60 respondents, they were asked what factors would discourage them from joining CityCycle, if they were in the process of considering membership. For each of the possible reasons offered, respondents were asked to provide a score (0–4), in terms of the degree to which the factor acted as a deterrent to using the bike share program. Illustrated in Figure 9.2, the results show that the most powerful barrier is not even directly about the bike share program itself; it's the convenience of driving. This highlights a very important point. People do not make decisions to use bike share in isolation from the other transport modes available to them. For Brisbane, the car is still very often the most convenient method of travel, especially for trips outside the Central Business District.

In 2014, Seattle launched a docked bike share program known as Pronto. Given the relatively supportive environment for cycling in Seattle, the failure of Pronto after just 3 years offers an interesting case study on bike share mismanagement. A complex set of factors led to the demise of this scheme of 500 bicycles and 50 docking stations. Pronto's small size limited the network benefits that can come from larger schemes. The docking stations were largely restricted to the downtown area and this, coupled with helmet requirements, and operator mismanagement and potential conflicts of interest have been cited as reasons for Pronto's failure. The director of the Seattle Department of Transportation was a former President of Alta Bike Share, the company operating Pronto. This resulted in a fine of $10,000 for failing to declare a conflict of interest.

Figure 9.2 If you were considering joining CityCycle, to what extent would these factors discourage you?
Source: Fishman et al. (2015). Other important barriers to CityCycle identified in Figure 9.2 were safety issues, and docking stations not being close enough to people's home.

Financial difficulties led to a cancellation of a Phase 2 expansion of the system, and the funding was instead directed towards improved bicycle infrastructure. The City took ownership of Pronto, but ridership continued to reduce and by March 2017, Pronto shut down.

Following the closure of Pronto, the City Council granted permits to three dockless bike share operators (LimeBike, Spin, and Ofo) on a trial basis. Each operator was initially allowed to launch with 1,000 bikes, with the cap gradually increasing to 4,000 each. Ridership for bike share services in Seattle has reportedly grown beyond Pronto's previous figures as a result. The experience of bike share in Seattle highlights the importance of careful planning, the need for good governance, and the importance of providing a scheme large enough to meet people's mobility needs. Finally, what has happened in Seattle since the demise of Pronto illustrates the current willingness of the private sector to provide bike share without government funding.

9.3 Bicycle Infrastructure

As mentioned in Chapter 1, rights of way are one of three crucial components of a transport system (Shoup, 2005). Third-generation bike share, by default, satisfies the first two requirements, that is, terminal capacity (docking stations) and vehicles (bicycles). Rights of way, in the form of bicycle lanes and paths can have a powerful impact on the popularity of bike share (Buck & Buehler, 2011).

The fear of collision with a motor vehicle is a major barrier to bicycle riding in general (Bauman et al., 2008; Garrard, 2009; Götschi, Garrard, & Giles-Corti, 2015; Rissel et al., 2010) and separated/protected bicycle infrastructure is shown to reduce perceptions of risk (Fishman, 2014).

In a study with three groups of participants, survey respondents were shown images of three bicycle riding environments (separated on-street bike lane, painted bike lane and no bike infrastructure) and asked to rate how safe they would feel riding in these environments. The three groups of participants were the following:

- Annual members of MBS
- Annual members of CityCycle
- A group with no known connection with bike share, identified as InSPiRS Panel in Figure 9.3.

The results indicate the majority, across all sample groups would feel safe or very safe riding on separated bicycle infrastructure, which is consistent with previous research (Wardman, Tight, & Page, 2007) as well as research conducted since this 2014 study (CDM Research & ASDF Research, 2017). By contrast, when presented with no bicycle infrastructure, an overwhelming proportion of respondents, across all groups, reported feeling very unsafe or unsafe, as illustrated in Figure 9.4. Whilst the level of bicycle infrastructure has improved in Melbourne and Brisbane over recent years, substantial areas within the MBS and CityCycle catchment have no bicycle infrastructure and the infrastructure that does exist is frequently disconnected, with the exception of waterway paths. These data may have implications for the ability of the MBS and CityCycle programs to attract those who currently do not ride.

The results shown in Figures 9.3 and 9.4 serve to highlight the difference in safety perceptions between those that do not ride, or do so infrequently (InSPiRS Panel) and bike share members (Fishman et al., 2015).

Whilst both Melbourne and Brisbane have progressively improved bicycle infrastructure provision over the last decade, more should have been done leading up to bike share's launch to create an environment that actively lowered the perception of risk, particularly for non- and infrequent bicycle riders. At the time of launch, each city only had one on-road protected bicycle lane within the entire catchment, and many streets had no formal bicycle infrastructure, including on roads with fast moving, heavy volumes of motor vehicle traffic. These conditions are well known to deter people from cycling and increase both perceived and actual risk of collision (Fishman, Washington, & Haworth, 2012b; Götschi et al., 2015; Zahabi, Chang, Miranda-Moreno, & Patterson, 2016).

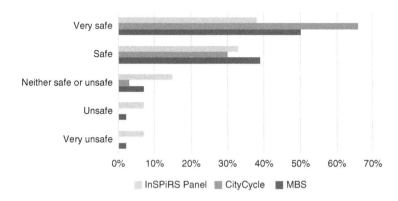

Figure 9.3 How safe do you feel riding on a separated lane/path?
Source: Fishman (2014).

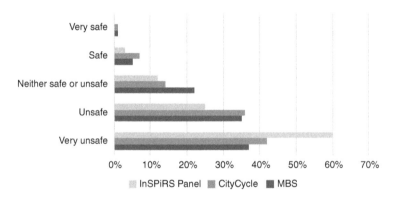

Figure 9.4 How safe do you feel when riding on road with no bike lane?
Source: Fishman (2014).

9.4 CityCycle Sign-Up Procedures

During CityCycle's crucial introductory phase (when public intrigue was at its highest), substantial delays were encountered by those wishing to join. A short-term, casual user seeking to sign up via the telephone was required to spend up to 25 minutes, listening to seven pages of terms and conditions before being granted access to the system (Fishman, 2014). Long-term subscribers typically waited three business days before being able to use the bikes. Even after these procedures had been relaxed, in August 2011, there was a perception that these lengthy procedures were still in place. The first months of a bike share program represents a critical phase determining enduring public perceptions.

9.5 Catchment Size

Melbourne's bike share program in particular is at the global extreme in terms of the size of its bike share catchment relative to the size of the city, both in geographical and population terms. The former Chicago Transportation Commissioner Gabe Klein, explaining bike share, said 'I knew that any sort of nodal business was only as effective as the number of nodes you have' (Vanderbilt, 2013). The New York City Department of Transportation, in a lengthy investigation of the applicability of bike share for that city reached a similar conclusion to Klein, noting 'Evidence from bike-share programs around the world suggests that small programs do not provide meaningful transportation, health or economic development gains nor do they provide a significant basis from which the city could evaluate the effectiveness of the program' (New York City Department of City Planning, 2009, p. 100).

The level of utility (or satisfaction/usefulness) is dependent, to some degree, on the size of the docking station catchment area, as this is what largely governs where one is able to travel. The results shown in Figure 9.2 demonstrate the strong positive influence living or working in close proximity to a docking station can have on bike share membership (e.g., see Fishman et al., 2015). Similarly, proximity to docking stations featured strongly when non-members were asked what would encourage them to consider joining CityCycle. Melbourne's bike share catchment is among the world's smallest, on a people per bike basis, with less than 600 bicycles and five million people. A system on this scale fails to offer significant convenience or mobility enhancement, particularly given that it is competing with among the densest, most well connected and frequent public transport opportunities in Australia, including the centre of the world's largest tram/streetcar network.

A key lesson for other cities planning bike share is that the catchment must be large enough to offer a compelling value proposition to potential users. Central to this value proposition must be travel time competitiveness, whereby for some trips, bike share should be the fastest form of travel between two points.

9.6 Launch Season

Bike share programs typically launch in spring or summer, when conditions are generally most conducive to bicycling. As previously indicated, launching MBS at the beginning of winter may have had a significant negative impact on usage levels (Brennan, 2013, 8 May, Personal communication regarding the impacts of winter start date on MBS). There is certainly evidence that winter weather reduces private bicycle usage levels, even in Australia (Ahmed, Rose, & Jacob, 2010), and it is difficult to imagine how bike share would be immune to this effect. The winter start date of MBS meant bikes sat underused for the first 100 days or so of the program (each bike used approximately once every 3 days), until the weather became more conducive to riding. This served to reinforce a perception that the bikes were unpopular, which, as shown in focus groups conducted by the author (see Fishman, Washington, & Haworth, 2012a) can create a self-reinforcing downward spiral ('I don't see anyone using them, so I won't use them'). The public's attitude to bike share was formed in these early, critical months and has persisted, even in the face of change (e.g., easier access to helmets, warmer weather).

The clear implication from Melbourne's experience is to launch bike share to coincide with the beginning of the season most likely to bring weather conducive to bicycling. The importance of seeing others using bike share as a way of 'nudging' others is an important implication from studies examining poorly performing bike share programs (Fishman, 2014). The findings may assist in the development of promotional strategies, particularly in the form of measures intended to incentivise use, such as heavily discounted subscriptions for early adopters, subscribe a friend and both receive a discount, and other financial incentives designed to drive early uptake. Those responsible for marketing bike share programs may gain useful insights from examining the innovations ride sourcing services (e.g., Uber, Lyft) have been using to encourage subscribers to access their social network to join.

9.7 Bike Share and Mandatory Helmet Requirements

As introduced earlier, mandatory helmet legislation (MHL) has reduced usage levels of both the Melbourne and Brisbane bike share programs. The deterrent effect of MHL is most powerful when no effective strategies have been developed prior to launch.

The 2010 launch of bike share in Brisbane and Melbourne was accompanied by considerable public intrigue. Members of the public would commonly approach the docking station, touch one of the bikes, perhaps ring the bell or play with the handlebars, ponder the information display, turn and walk away. The author was in both cities at the time of launch and witnessed this series of events repeatedly. Moreover, even those that did end up joining either scheme report using bike share less due to MHL (Fishman, 2014; Fishman & Schepers, 2016). By the time helmets were placed on the bicycles themselves, public intrigue with bike share had largely evaporated (Fishman, 2014). Neither city conducted a detailed examination of how MHL might impact bike share usage, and no effective measures were in place to minimise the negative impact associated with these regulations on bike share. Some 12 months after the establishment of CityCycle, a decision was made to place helmets on the bicycles themselves, and this appears to have led to an increase in casual usage, although the change coincided with lower usage fees. In early 2013, MBS adopted a similar approach, although many of the MBS helmets are used by people riding their own private bicycles.

The current Active Transport Chairman at Brisbane City Council, Cr Adrian Schrinner has said that MHL is the biggest impediment to higher CityCycle usage (Atfield, 2016b).

The impact of MHL on bike share use is not restricted to Australian cities. In Seattle, Washington, which also has MHL, their now defunct docked bike share program (Pronto) has been criticised for low usage levels (only slightly higher than Melbourne's). In early 2017, when Seattle closed their bike share program, some attributed the helmet laws as contributing to the demise of this program. This led the former NYC Transportation Commissioner, Janet Sadik Khan to tweet: 'NYC has no helmet law, 38 million bike share trips and 0 deaths[2]. Seattle has a helmet law and 1 dead bike share system.' Seattle's docked bike share scheme has been re-placed by a number of dockless bike share operators, and it is understood their mandatory helmet law is not strictly enforced.

Tel Aviv and Mexico City both repealed their mandatory helmet laws to make way for bike share (Sadik-Khan & Solomonow, 2016).

MHL hampers the spontaneity with which people are able to use bike share. The public have shown a strong aversion to carrying a helmet with them should they choose to use bike share at some point during the day (Fishman et al., 2012a). Focus groups conducted in Perth, Australia, in 2016 revealed a reluctance to share helmets, due to hygiene concerns, backing up similar findings from an earlier study (Fishman et al., 2012a). There will also be some people that object to wearing a helmet even if its cleanliness is assured, for 'hairstyle preservation' reasons. Thus, even with the provision of freely accessible helmets on the bicycles themselves, and even if sanitised, helmets continue to act as a deterrent to bike share. To date, the author is unable to find an example in which a city with MHL also has a successful bike share program.

9.7.1 Helmet Use in Bike Share Systems Without Helmet Laws

In cities with voluntary helmet use, observational studies have found bike share riders are four times less likely to wear helmets than private bike rid-ers in the same city, controlling for age and gender (Fischer et al., 2012). Similarly, in Washington, D.C., studies have found that casual bike share users are much less likely to wear helmets than long-term subscribers, al-though in both groups the majority of those surveyed report not wearing helmets (Buck et al., 2013). Some 85% of Citi Bike riders in New York City do not wear a helmet (Basch, Zagnit, Rajan, Ethan, & Basch, 2014). It is suspected that the key reason for the consistent finding that bike share users are less inclined to wear helmets is because bike share use often is just one leg of multiple modes people make throughout the day, and most people do not regard carrying a helmet with them as a realistic option. The more spontaneous a bike share journey is, the less likely a helmet will be worn.

9.7.2 What Should a City with Helmet Laws Do If It Wishes to Start a Bike Share Program?

The evidence very clearly shows that MHL have a negative impact on bike share use, with members indicating they use bike share less than they would if helmet use was voluntary (Fishman, 2014). This in itself is not a sufficient reason to repeal the legislation, as some have suggested. The efficacy of MHL on overall population health is a topic of considerable debate, and any adjustment to MHL must consider the overall impact on population health.

Given the weight of evidence that MHL limits bike share use, cities with MHL that are also interested in establishing a bike share program should consider undertaking an investigation of the overall population health impact of a MHL waiver for bike share use. This study should be focused on determining the following:

- The conditions under which a waiver might operate. Would it only encompass bike share riders, or all riders? Should it only apply to riding under certain conditions (e.g., contingent on high quality bicycle infrastructure, speed/volume of motor vehicle traffic). Would it only apply to adults, or children as well?
- If a waiver were to be introduced, what percentage of current riders would continue to wear a helmet and might this vary depending on conditions? Some riders might wear a helmet when riding on busy roads but go helmet free on shared paths. Answers to this question are necessary to help determine the risk profile of riders.
- How much new cycling would occur should a waiver be introduced and how much physical activity were those people doing prior to the waiver? Has this new cycling replaced other forms of physical activity (e.g., now that they are cycling, are they not going to the gym or some other form of physical activity?).
- Whether the healthy life years[3] lost to forecast new head injuries is greater than the healthy life years gained through additional physical activity from riding that occurs because of the mandatory helmet waiver.

The above research questions are highly complex, and there are multiple feedback loops that may have an important influence on the result. A multi-disciplinary study team is needed that includes road safety and population health experts. The study should also include modelling of the impacts of changes to bicycle infrastructure and speed limits, as it may be these elements that are crucial to overall population health outcomes.

Should the outcome of this investigation find that a waiver to MHL is likely to result in more healthy life years lost (in the form of head injury) compared to the number of healthy life years gained due to increased physical activity, a waiver may not be advisable.

It is also important to recognise that one of the strongest arguments in favour of an investigation of the impacts of a MHL waiver for bike share use is the higher levels of safety associated with riding a bike share bike. As highlighted in Section 4.3, bike share bikes are typically slower, more upright, sturdier and are fitted with full-time safety lights. Their usage has a much higher safety record than private bikes, on a per kilometre travelled basis (Fishman & Schepers, 2016). There is no reason these findings should not be taken into account when determining an appropriate response to MHLs.

It must be stressed that the need to undertake a study of this type is not recommending a waiver to MHL, rather it is to examine the likely impact of a waiver through a modelling study focused on comparing probable population health outcomes. Finally, any waiver of MHL for bike share use should be accompanied by a similar helmet use encouragement strategy employed in many other cities (e.g., New York City, San Francisco, Chicago). This should include substantial discounts for helmet purchase and other promotional activities.

9.8 Summary of Lessons Learnt from Australia's Experience with Bike Share

In the 8 years since the establishment of Australia's two docked bike share programs, usage levels have failed to approach that of international norms and no other Australian city has established a docked bike share program. This is partly due to apprehension arising from low usage in Melbourne and Brisbane. Brisbane, after several years of very poor usage, has recently made some enhancements to its pricing and access policies, and this been associated with greater take-up. This serves to highlight the importance of launching bike share with a low price and spontaneous sign-up options.

This section offers a distillation of the key factors that contributed to the low usage levels that have characterised both Australian schemes.

- Small catchment: Particularly for Melbourne, the catchment is very small compared to the size of Melbourne and has among the lowest ratios of bikes per person of any bike share program globally. Small systems fail to provide the network of origins and destinations to attract a wide group of users.

  The small scale of MBS failed to offer significant convenience or mobility benefits to potential users, particularly given that in its location, it is competing with some of the densest, most well-connected and frequent public transport services in Australia. Moreover, public transport ticketing in Melbourne is structured such that if one enters and plans to leave the downtown area by public transport, there is no additional cost for an unlimited amount of central city travel during the day. Ensuring public transport complements rather than competes with public transport is another lesson highlighted by MBS. No attempt was made to integrate bike share access with Melbourne's public transport ticketing, despite evidence showing the importance this provides from a user experience perspective (Fishman et al., 2012a).

- Sign-up difficulty in Brisbane: The process prospective CityCycle users were required to undertake had a detrimental and lasting impact on usage (Fishman et al., 2012a). Unlike most modern bike share programs, users were unable to sign up on the spot via a credit card swipe at a payment kiosk. For more than a year after the launch of CityCycle, prospective users were required to call a number, during office hours, to manually sign up to the program. With most bike share trips being under 16 minutes, it appears members of the public were unwilling to wait the time required to make their first trip. Finally, for the first 2 years, members were locked out of the system between 10 pm and 5 am, and this, in addition to the aforementioned issues were key frustrations for members (Fishman et al., 2012a; Roy Morgan Research, 2013) that ultimately impacted on their wiliness to renew membership. This was a lost opportunity that failed to capitalise on the interest people had in trying Brisbane's bike share program. Whilst the sign-up process has been somewhat streamlined, and the user fees substantially reduced, the reputation damage this had on CityCycle's 'brand' may have had a lasting impact on ridership.

- Launch in winter: As highlighted earlier, MBS was launched in May, the beginning of cooler weather, which is well known to reduce cycling participation (Ahmed, Rose, Figliozzi, & Jakob, 2012). This resulted in less usage in the crucial first few months of the program. On average, each bike sat unused for around 72 hours (one ride per 3 days) in the introductory months of the program. People became accustomed to seeing the bicycles sitting unused, and therefore, even when the weather improved, the public perception was that 'people don't use MBS'. The best advertisement for bike share is seeing other people using it, and this is something all cities seeking to establish bike share must recognise.

- No helmet plan: As described earlier in this chapter, no effective strategies were in place at the time of launch to allow those intrigued by bike share to immediately use the program. By the time such strategies had been developed, the intrigue had evaporated and people typically walked past docking stations, without noticing the newly added helmets. The experience from Brisbane and Melbourne demonstrates why it is important to deploy considerable research, planning and implementation activities to mitigate the barrier presented by MHL. This investigation should also be open to a range of possible measures, including an examination of the impacts of introducing a waiver to helmet requirements for bike share use. The safety benefits of bike share compared to private bicycle riding are compelling (e.g., see Fishman & Schepers, 2016; Martin, Cohen, Botha, & Shaheen, 2016), and therefore, the population health impacts of a helmet waiver for bike share is a question that is yet to be addressed in the empirical literature.

- Limited bicycle infrastructure: The bicycle infrastructure network is far from complete in Melbourne (more than 60% of the Principal Bicycle Network is 'proposed') and is even less mature in Brisbane. Safety issues remain one of the most significant deterrents to cycling in Melbourne (Pucher, Greaves, & Garrard, 2010) and Brisbane (Fishman et al., 2012a). In many cities that have established well-used bike share programs (e.g., Barcelona, New York City, Paris), the dedicated program of bicycle network expansion occurred in the years leading up to launching a bike share program. Melbourne and Brisbane launched bike share without a sufficient network of protected bicycle infrastructure to support strong usage levels.

- Free tram zone/ticketing system in Melbourne: At the beginning of 2015, Melbourne introduced a free tram zone within its CBD. This has caused a rise in tram patronage and informal discussion between the author and the bike share operator suggest that bike share usage has reduced since the introduction of the free tram zone.

- Limited marketing/promotional activity: Compared to bike share programs in other cities, Australian bike share programs have been under active in relation to marketing. Other cities have run free 'come and try days', closed off inner city streets for training events, offered two for one deals and other initiatives to incentivise usage. MBS and CityCycle's social media activities have also been modest compared to many other bike share programs.

Notes

1 This is the Greater Melbourne and Brisbane populations, as defined by the Australian Bureau of Statistics. See http://www.abs.gov.au/ausstats/abs@.nsf/mf/3218.0
2 In June 2017, Citi Bike recorded its first fatality.
3 An indicator used in epidemiology to measure the number of remaining years a person of a certain age is still supposed to live without disability. See http://ec.europa.eu/health/indicators/healthy_life_years/hly_en

References

Ahmed, F., Rose, G., Figliozzi, M., & Jakob, C. (2012). *Commuter cyclist's sensitivity to changes in weather: Insight from two cities with different climatic conditions.* Paper presented at the Transportation Research Board Annual Meeting, Washington, DC.
Ahmed, F., Rose, G., & Jacob, C. (2010). *Impact of weather on commuter cyclist behaviour and implications for climate change adaptation.* Paper presented at the Australasian Transport Research Forum, Canberra.

Alta Bike Share. (2011). *Melbourne Bike Share Survey.* Melbourne: Alta Bike Share.

Atfield, C. (2016a). Brisbane Deputy Mayor Adrian Schrinner backs voluntary helmet trial for cyclists. *Sydney Morning Herald.* Retrieved from http://www. smh.com.au/federal-politics/political-news/brisbane-deputy-mayor-adrian-schrinner-backs-voluntary-helmet-trial-for-cyclists-20160503-gokuha.html

Atfield, C. (2016b). Mayor defends cost of Brisbane's CityCycle scheme. *Brisbane Times.* Retrieved from http://www.brisbanetimes.com.au/queensland/mayor-defends-cost-of-brisbanes-citycycle-scheme-20160607-gpdx6a.html

Basch, C. H., Zagnit, E. A., Rajan, S., Ethan, D., & Basch, C. E. (2014). Helmet use among cyclists in New York City. *Journal of Community Health, 39,* 1–3.

Bauman, A. E., Rissel, C., Garrard, J., Ker, I., Speidel, R., & Fishman, E. (2008). Cycling: Getting Australia Moving: Barriers, Facilitators and Interventions to Get More Australians Physically Active through Cycling. Retrieved from https://sensibletransport.org.au/wp-content/uploads/2015/08/CPF-Cycling-Getting-Australia-Moving-Report-Updated-2009.pdf.

Buck, D., & Buehler, R. (2011). *Bike lanes and other determinants of Capital Bikeshare Trips.* Paper presented at the Transportation Research Board Annual Meeting 2012, Washington, DC. Conference paper retrieved from http://ralphbu.files. wordpress.com/2012/02/buck-buehler-poster-cabi-trb-2012.pdf

Buck, D., Buehler, R., Happ, P., Rawls, B., Chung, P. P., & Borecki, N. (2013). Are bikeshare users different from regular cyclists? *Transportation Research Record: Journal of the Transportation Research Board, 2387*(1), 112–119.

CDM Research & ASDF Research. (2017). Near-market Research. Retrieved from Melbourne: https://journals.sagepub.com/doi/10.3141/2387-13

Fischer, C. M., Sanchez, C. E., Pittman, M., Milzman, D., Volz, K. A., Huang, H., … Sanchez, L. D. (2012). Prevalence of bicycle helmet use by users of public bikeshare programs. *Annals of Emergency Medicine, 60*(2), 228–231.

Fishman, E. (2012). Fixing Australian Bike Share Goes beyond Helmet Laws. Retrieved from https://theconversation.edu.au/fixing-australian-bike-share-goes-beyond-helmet-laws-10229

Fishman, E. (2014). *Bikeshare: Barriers, facilitators and impacts on car use* (PhD thesis by publication). Queensland University of Technology, Brisbane.

Fishman, E. (2015). Bikeshare: A review of recent literature. *Transport Reviews,* 1–22. doi:10.1080/01441647.2015.1033036

Fishman, E., & Schepers, P. (2016). Global bike share: What the data tells us about road safety. *Journal of Safety Research, 56,* 41–45.

Fishman, E., Washington, S., & Haworth, N. (2012a). Barriers and facilitators to public bicycle scheme use: A qualitative approach. *Transportation Research Part F-Traffic Psychology and Behaviour, 15*(6), 686–698.

Fishman, E., Washington, S., & Haworth, N. (2012b). Understanding the fear of bicycle riding in Australia. *Journal of the Australasian College of Road Safety, 23*(3), 19–27.

Fishman, E., Washington, S., Haworth, N., & Mazzei, A. (2014). Barriers to bikesharing: An analysis from Melbourne and Brisbane. *Journal of Transport Geography, 41,* 325–337.

Fishman, E., Washington, S., Haworth, N., & Watson, A. (2015). Factors influencing bike share membership: An analysis of Melbourne and Brisbane. *Transportation Research Part A, 71,* 17–30. doi:10.1016/j.tra.2014.10.021

Garrard, J. (2009). Active Transport: Adults: An Overview of Recent Evidence. Retrieved from Melbourne: https://www.vichealth.vic.gov.au/-/media/ResourceCentre/PublicationsandResources/Active-travel/Active_Transport_Adults_FINAL.pdf?la=en&hash=B7BEDE09B12F8E8A4ADD49858DB2578CD33B2B7A

Götschi, T., Garrard, J., & Giles-Corti, B. (2015). Cycling as a part of daily life: A review of Health Perspectives. *Transport Reviews*, 1–27. doi:10.1080/01441647.2015.1057877

Gutman, D. (2016). Will Helmet Law Kill Seattle's New Bike-share Program? Retrieved from http://www.seattletimes.com/seattle-news/transportation/will-helmet-law-kill-seattles-new-bike-share-program/

Haworth, N., Schramm, A., King, M., & Steinhardt, D. (2010). Bicycle Helmet Research. Retrieved from http://eprints.qut.edu.au/41798/1/Monograph_5.pdf

Martin, E., Cohen, A., Botha, J., & Shaheen, S. (2016). Bikesharing and Bicycle Safety. Retrieved from San Jose: http://transweb.sjsu.edu/PDFs/research/1204-bikesharing-and-bicycle-safety.pdf

Médard de Chardon, C., Caruso, G., & Thomas, I. (2017). Bicycle sharing system 'success' determinants. *Transportation Research Part A: Policy and Practice, 100*, 202–214.

New York City Department of City Planning. (2009). Bike-share: Opportunities in New York City. Retrieved from https://www1.nyc.gov/assets/planning/download/pdf/plans/transportation/bike_share_complete.pdf

Pucher, J., Greaves, S., & Garrard, J. (2010). Cycling Down Under: A Comparative Analysis of Bicycling Trends and Policies in Sydney and Melbourne. *Journal of Transport Geography, 19*(2), 332–345.

Rissel, C., Merom, D., Bauman, A., Garrard, J., Wen, L. M., & New, C. (2010). Current cycling, bicycle path use, and willingness to cycle more-findings from a community survey of cycling in Southwest Sydney, Australia. *Journal of Physical Activity & Health, 7*(2), 267–272.

Roy Morgan Research. (2013). Brisbane City Council CityCycle Customer Satisfaction Research. Retrieved from Brisbane.

Sadik-Khan, J., & Solomonow, S. (2016). *Streetfight: Handbook for an Urban Revolution*. New York: Viking.

Shoup, D. (2005). *The High Cost of Free Parking*. Chicago, IL: Planners Press.

Vanderbilt, T. (2013). The best bike-sharing program in the United States. *Slate.com*. Retrieved from http://www.slate.com/articles/life/doers/2013/01/capital_bikeshare_how_paul_demaio_gabe_klein_adrian_fenty_and_other_dc_leaders.html

Ward, C. (2011). Two in three CityCycle bikes sitting idle. In *Brisbane Times*. Retrieved from https://www.brisbanetimes.com.au/national/queensland/two-in-three-citycycle-bikes-sitting-idle-20110512-1ek9r.html

Zahabi, S. A. H., Chang, A., Miranda-Moreno, L. F., & Patterson, Z. (2016). Exploring the link between the neighborhood typologies, bicycle infrastructure and commuting cycling over time and the potential impact on commuter GHG emissions. *Transportation Research Part D: Transport and Environment, 47*, 89–103. doi:10.1016/j.trd.2016.05.008

10 Factors Determining Bike Share Use

The benefits of bike share are directly related to the degree that bike share is used. The number of trips per day, per bike is an increasingly recognised method of comparing bike share systems in terms of performance (Médard de Chardon, Caruso, & Thomas, 2017). Overall, studies that have sought to measure the impact of various factors on bike share use have found that the quality of bicycle infrastructure, station density, population density and the degree of difficulty driving a car are all important variables (Buck & Buehler, 2011; Fishman, 2015; Médard de Chardon et al., 2017). Whilst it is generally accepted that large bike share systems offer 'network benefits' that result in increased usage (e.g., see Institute for Transportation & Development Policy, 2018), some researchers have found it difficult to identify a strong statistical relationship between the overall size of a bike share scheme and usage (Médard de Chardon et al., 2017). It is likely that size is an important factor, but it is not the *only* important factor. Overall, a combination of factors influencing transport decisions in general will have an impact on bike share. As identified in earlier, people do not make decisions to use bike share in isolation. Therefore, a complex mix of influences; some related to the design of the bike share scheme itself (e.g., density of stations, price of service) and others related to the city more generally (e.g., urban density, quality of other transport options) are important determinants of bike share use. This chapter explores some of the research examining the factors determining bike share usage levels.

A study conducted between 2012 and 2013 found some significant differences between those signed up as bike share members and those who had not, but lived in a city with bike share. The results, published in *Transportation Research Part A* (see Fishman, Washington, Haworth, & Watson, 2015) revealed that bike share members were significantly younger, more likely to know the distance between their home and work to their closest docking station, have pre-tax incomes above A$104,000 per annum and have friends or family who are bike share members. Moreover, bike share members were considerably more likely to have ridden a bicycle in the month prior to undertaking the survey. Bike share members were also disproportionately male, and this is generally consistent with previous research showing higher cycling levels among males in Australia (Pucher, Greaves, & Garrard, 2010) and the United States (Pucher, Buehler, & Seinen, 2011).

Table 10.1 presents some of similarities and variations between sample groups, and a comparison with Census data for Greater Melbourne and Greater Brisbane is provided where possible.

As identified in Table 10.1, the most frequent age range from the Census is somewhat younger than bike share groups, and considerably younger than the non-member Panel. This may reflect the fact that respondents to this study were required to be 18 years or older. When removing those under 18 years from the Census data, the distribution of age ranges show considerable similarity between bike share groups. Bike share members are more heavily represented within the 25–44 age band. By contrast, the non-member Panel shows a larger proportion within the 50–64 age brackets. Those aged 60 and over are under-represented as bike share members, which is consistent with the findings of other researchers on bike share (LDA Consulting, 2013; Shaheen, Martin, Cohen, & Finson, 2012; Virginia Tech, 2012) as well as private cycling in North America (Pucher et al., 2011).

The highest level of education varied considerably between sample groups, and these groups differed substantially from Greater Melbourne and Greater Brisbane Census data. As shown in Figure 10.1, bike share members achieved higher education levels than both the non-member group and the general population in both cities. For instance, some 81% and 77% of *MBS* and *CityCycle* members, respectively, have Bachelor's Degree or higher, compared to 50% for the non-member group and 22% and 18% for Greater Melbourne and Greater Brisbane. Previous research has found similar results with respect to the educational attainment of bike share users (Shaheen et al., 2012).

Respondents were asked their main mode of transport for their most recent journey to work. The results indicate that around one fifth of

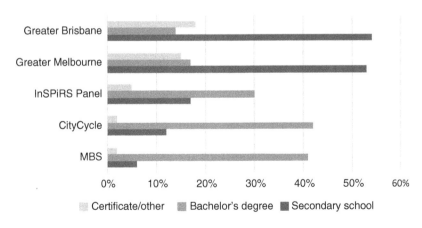

Figure 10.1 Highest education level.
Source: Fishman et al. (2015), Greater Melbourne and Greater Brisbane (Australian Bureau of Statistics, 2013).
NB: Greater Melbourne and Greater Brisbane included anyone over 15 years old, whereas sample groups were restricted to those over 18 years old.

Table 10.1 Differences between bike share members and non-members

Variable		Melbourne Bike Share	CityCycle	Non-member (InSPiRS Panel)	Greater Melbourne[a]	Greater Brisbane[a]
Most frequent age range		30–34 (16.9%)	30–34 (16.6%)	55–59 (19.8%)	25–29 (7.9%)	25–29 (7.6%)
Male		N = 285 (76.6%)	N = 265 (59.8%)	N = 25 (41.7%)	49.2%	49.3%
Female		N = 87 (23.4%)	N = 178 (40.2%)	N = 35 (58.3%)	50.8%	50.7%
Mean distance between home and work		10.7 km (SD 9.5)	8.6 km (SD 7.7)	13.2 km (SD 10.4)	10 km[d]	15.3 km[c]
Percentage living within 500 m of a docking station		44%	54.1%	5%[b]	NA	NA
Percentage working within 500 m of a docking station		83.9%	83.6%	15%[b]	NA	NA
Annual income range	Less than $41,599	7.6%	14.9%	21.7%	56.8%	55.4%
	$41,600–$77,999	20.0%	28.0%	48.3%	22.6%	24.0%
	$78,000–$103,999	19.2%	22.3%	15.0%	6.4%	7.0%
	$104,000 or more	43.0%	26.9%	5.0%	6.5%	6.3%
	No response	10.3%	7.9%	10.0%	7.6%	7.2%
Car ownership		76.6%	80.4%	100%	NA	NA
Free car park at work		19.9%	26%	63.3%	NA	NA
Mean number of family/friends who are bike share members		0.59 (SD 0.87)	0.95 (SD 1.10)	0.05 (SD 0.28)	NA	NA
Most frequently reported bicycle riding activity in past month		16+ trips (35.8%)	16+ trips (33%)	No bicycle riding activity (75%)	NA	NA

Source: Fishman et al. (2015).
a   Australian Bureau of Statistics (2013).
b   Approximately 50% of InSPiRS members responded "Don't know" in relation to the distance between their home and work and closest docking station.
c   ABS 2006 Census, for South East Queensland (Doonan, 2010).
d   ABS 2011 Census, reporting median distance (Department of Infrastructure and Transport, 2013).

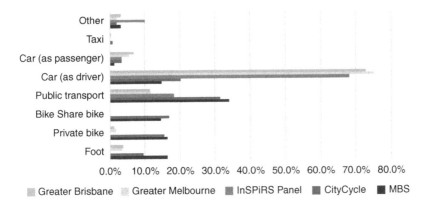

Figure 10.2 Mode for most recent journey to work.
Source: Fishman et al. (2015), Greater Melbourne and Greater Brisbane (Australian Bureau of Statistics, 2013).

bike share members used bike share as their main mode, with a similar proportion travelling on a private bike. By contrast, Census data reveal that private bike travel constitutes the main mode in less than 2% of trips in both Greater Melbourne and Greater Brisbane. No non–bike share group members (referred to as the InSPiRS Panel in Figure 10.2) nominated either public or private bikes as their main mode to work on the day the survey was undertaken. Full results are shown in Figure 10.2.

10.1 Why Members Use Bike Share

Limited research has been undertaken on the personal motivations for those choosing to use bike share. *Capital Bikeshare* in Washington, D.C. have consistently sought to gauge the reasons why people use their system. The latest study, published in 2017, found that 90% of respondents joined to assist them in getting around more easily and quickly (LDA Consulting, 2017). Just over 50% of respondents said that Capital Bikeshare is *faster* than other modes of transport. Another key finding from Washington, D.C. that is consistent with other cities is that members report using bike share because it makes integration with other modes easier. Being able to make one way bike trips and then using another mode when it is more convenient is valued by members (LDA Consulting, 2017). Similarly, users of the London Cycle Hire Scheme indicated that its ease of use and convenience, as well as cost-effectiveness were key reasons for membership (Transport for London, 2018).

In 2012, all annual *Melbourne Bike Share* (MBS) members were invited to take part in a survey relating to their bike share usage. The ~350 respondents were asked why they had joined *MBS*, requiring them to

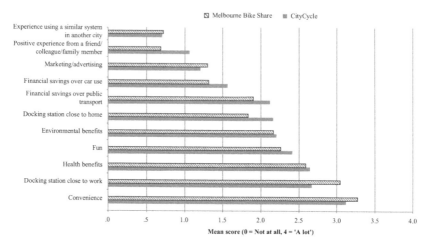

Figure 10.3 Why people use bike share.
Source: Fishman et al. (2014).

nominate the degree to which the factors shown in Figure 10.3 influenced their motivation for bike share. The results indicate that *convenience* is the most powerful motivator, and this is consistent with results from London and Washington, D.C. reported earlier. Having a docking station close to work was the second most powerful motivator (which is also broadly captured within the *convenience* motivation).

Other research has shown the importance of docking station proximity to *home*. For instance, Bachand-Marleau, Lee and El-Geneidy (2012) found Montreal respondents living within 500 metres of a docking station were 3.2 times more likely to have used bike share. One possible explanation for why this did not emerge from the Australian research is that the docking station catchment is overwhelmingly located in *employment* rather than *residential* districts, and this is especially so for Melbourne (Fishman, Washington, Haworth, & Mazzei, 2014).

10.1.1 Factors That Encourage Non-bike Share Uses to Sign Up

As previously identified, it has proved difficult for researchers to receive responses regarding bike share barriers from those without a pre-existing interest in bike share (Fishman, 2014). A pre-existing survey Panel (known as the InSPiRS Panel) was asked what would *encourage* them to consider becoming a bike share member. Factors related to *safety* and *convenience* emerged as the strongest encouragement factors. *More bike lanes and paths* and *automatically open to GoCard*[1] *holders* receiving the strongest mean scores.

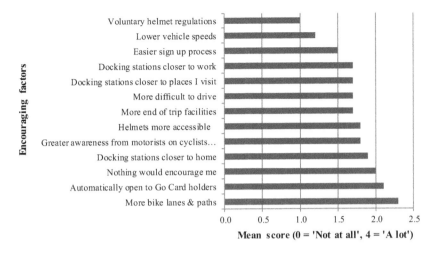

Figure 10.4 To what extent would these factors encourage you to become a CityCycle member?
Source: Fishman et al. (2015).

Figure 10.4 provides a summary of the responses to those who had not joined *CityCycle* in Brisbane but were asked what measures might encourage them to do so. More bike lanes and paths were considered the most important measure Brisbane could take to encourage ridership.

10.1.2 Predictors of Bike Share Membership in Australia

In previous research, statistical analysis (binary logistic regression) was conducted using the results of surveys on bike share members in Australia (Fishman et al., 2015) and a group with no known connection to bike share (all non-members and referred to as the InSPiRS Panel). The pertinent findings of this study relating to *MBS* are summarised below (see Fishman et al., 2015).

Riding activity in the previous month was found to be a reliable predictor of bike share membership. Riding at least once in the previous month was associated with a 5.8-fold increase in the odds of being a bike share member compared to those who reported no bike riding in the month prior to undertaking the survey. This is generally consistent with previous research, which has found those who ride a private bike are more likely to be bike share members (Fishman, Washington, & Haworth, 2012; Fuller et al., 2011; Shaheen, Zhang, Martin, & Guzman, 2011). It is further supported by the notion that there are, in broad terms, two categories of barrier to bike share usage. The first relates to barriers to riding in general (such as safety perceptions or distance). The second concerns bike share–specific barriers (such as lack of close proximity to docking stations). By definition, regular bike riders have not found the first set of barriers insurmountable and therefore find fewer barriers to the use of bike share (Fishman et al., 2015).

The level of convenience respondents associated with private bike riding was found to be a significant predictor of bike share membership. Respondents were asked to what degree convenience acts as an encouragement to private bike riding, using a 1–5 scale from 'Not at all' to 'A lot'. Each increment towards 'A lot' increased the odds of bike share membership 1.9-fold. This corresponds with research on motivation for public bike riding, with consultant reports on the *MBS* program (Alta Bike Share, 2011; Traffix Group, 2012), peer-reviewed research on the CityCycle scheme (Fishman et al., 2012) and North American research (Shaheen et al., 2012). Each body of work found convenience to be a key factor, motivating bike share membership and usage.

Those aged 18–34 had 3.3-fold greater odds of being a bike share member than all other age groups. Previous research has shown bike share members are typically younger than the general adult population (Fuller et al., 2011; LDA Consulting, 2012; Lewis, 2011; Transport for London, 2010). Income (pre-tax) was found to be a significant predictor of bike share membership. Each higher increment along a 10-point scale (less than $10,400 to $104,000+) was associated with a 1.3-fold increase in the odds of being a bike share member. This finding is generally consistent with a survey of London bike share members, which found users of the scheme to be disproportionately white, aged 25–44 and wealthy relative to the general London population (Transport for London, 2010).

Respondents who indicated they work within 250 m of a docking station had 29.9-fold greater odds of being a bike share member. Distance from docking station has been found by other researchers to be an important association with bike share membership. Fuller et al. (2011) investigated the prevalence of using the Montreal bike share scheme (known as *BIXI*) at least once depending on whether the subject lived within 250 m of at least one docking station. For those living within 250 m of a docking station, 14.3% of residents had used *BIXI*, whereas only 6% had when living greater than 250 m of a docking station. As shown in *Table 10.1,* bike share members were considerably more likely to work rather than live within 500 m of a docking station. This finding may be influenced by the configuration of the bike share docking station catchments, and this is especially so for Melbourne. As highlighted previously, the *MBS* program is particularly small relative to the size of the city (600 bikes and a Greater Melbourne population of 5 million). The docking stations are largely in the central employment district, rather than residential neighbourhoods. Therefore, the finding that distance between docking station and work was more powerful than the distance between home and docking station may be influenced by the current catchment configuration.

10.1.3 Application of the Logistic Regression Model

The logistic regression results are used to predict how changing variable values alter the odds of bike share membership. When variable values are held at their means, the probability of bike share membership is at or close to 0 – which broadly reflects the current usage of bike share in both Melbourne and Brisbane, in which only a very small proportion of the population are members. Nevertheless, as illustrated in some of the hypothetical scenarios below, it is possible to predict a relatively high probability of being a bike share member through the manipulation of key variables. The variable *Convenience as an encouraging factor for private bike riding*, in which respondents were asked to rate the level to which this statement is true (1 = Not at all, 5 = A lot) has been used as the horizontal axis in Figure 10.5, extrapolating the means, from 1 through to 5.

Income $104K+, work <250 m docking describes a scenario in which incomes are set at their highest level and the distance between place of work and closest docking station is within 250 m. In the second scenario, *Work*

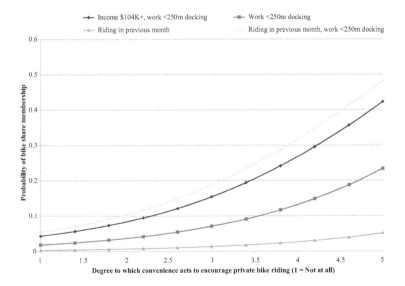

Figure 10.5 Probability of bike share membership under different scenarios, with convenience extended through its range of means.
Source: Fishman et al. (2015).

<250 m docking, the settings are the same as the previous scenario, with the exception of the income variable, which has been left at the mean. The third scenario in Figure 10.5 holds values at their mean, with the exception of *riding in the previous month*, which has been changed to 'yes'. The fourth scenario in Figure 10.5 is identical to the previous scenario, with one crucial addition; the distance between work and the closest docking station is now *within 250 m*. There is a considerable difference in the probability of bike share membership between these two scenarios, shown in Figure 10.5 and is indicative of the importance of proximity between workplace and docking station.

Figure 10.6 uses the variable of annual income on the horizontal axis, to predict bike share membership, with five scenarios shown.

Highest scenario + no riding previous month differs from previous scenarios in that the means for each variable have not been selected by default. In this scenario, the means have intentionally been adjusted to the values most typical of a bike share member. Should this procedure be carried out for all variables, the probability of being a bike share member rises to 1. For illustrative purposes, this scenario has adjusted the riding activity variable to equal 0 (no riding in previous month), with probabilities rising from 0.09 at the lowest income bracket ($10,400 or less) to 0.52 at the

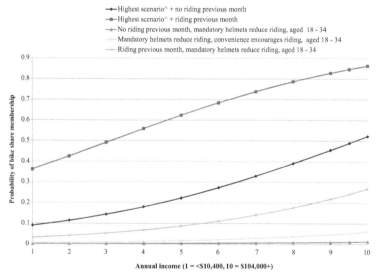

This scenario includes being aged between 18 and 34, working within 250 m of a docking station, convenience acting as a strong motivator for private bike riding, and mandatory helmets reducing bike riding.

Figure 10.6 Probability of bike share membership under different scenarios, with income extended through its range of means.

highest income level ($104,000+). *Highest scenario + riding previous month* can be understood based on the explanation of the previous scenario. Bike share membership probabilities rise from 0.36 to 0.86 from the lowest to highest income level. The difference between these two scenarios demonstrates the influence riding during the previous month has on increasing bike share membership probabilities.

Mandatory helmets reduce riding, convenience encourages riding, aged 18–34 illustrates a scenario in which the mandatory helmets variable has been adjusted to reduce riding and convenience has been adjusted to be a powerful motivator for riding a private bike (5 on a scale of 1–5). Moreover, the age category has been adjusted to include only those aged 18–34. The lowest income levels in this scenario shows a probability of bike share membership of 0.01, rising to 0.06 for the highest income bracket. The final scenario *No riding previous month, mandatory helmets reduce riding, aged 18–34* is similar to the previous scenario; however, *convenience* has been replaced with no riding during the previous month. This case provides the lowest probability of membership for the scenarios shown in Figure 10.6, reaching a maximum probability of 0.01 at the highest income bracket.

10.1.4 Conclusions

This chapter has analysed some of the research on the factors that influence bike share use. Unlike much of the other research on bike share, this chapter has included the findings from respondents who had no known connection with bike share. This is especially important for those focused on growing ridership levels. Understanding the barriers and facilitators to bike share, from those that are yet to use it is crucial to the success of any effort to increase ridership levels. The results of the study with Melbourne and Brisbane participants described in this chapter illustrate the magnitude of influence for various factors associated with bike share membership. The findings provide bike share operators and policy makers with an improved ability to influence membership levels. *Convenience* emerged as an important predictor of membership. Policy makers interested in expanding the membership base of bike share programs may benefit from designing bike share to be easily accessible. The distance to the closest docking station was found to be a predictor of membership, and this is consistent with previous research (Fuller et al., 2011; Molina-Garcia, Castillo, Queralt, & Sallis, 2013). This underscores the importance of planning a bike share system capable of providing the network benefits that provide a compelling proposition to citizens. Targeted expansion of docking stations, particularly around employment precincts and especially for those with large number of employees aged under 35 may provide a significant increase in membership.

The differences in safety perceptions between bike share members and non-members when presented with different levels of infrastructure provision (reported in Section 9.3) provide insights for bicycle infrastructure planners and those seeking to encourage bike share use. Specifically, non-members show lower levels of perceived safety in all bike-riding environments tested in this study. This suggests an expansion of the bicycle infrastructure network, particularly separated bicycle lanes, may be useful in growing bike share membership. Consistent with other research (e.g., see Médard de Chardon et al., 2017), the study reported in this chapter underlines the negative impact mandatory helmet legislation has on bike share usage.

Bike share members recorded significantly higher incomes than other groups. This is influenced, at least in part, by the current position of docking stations, in central Melbourne and Brisbane. Research using Census data shows that inner city residents have higher average incomes than those who reside in outer suburbs in Melbourne (Fishman & Brennan, 2010). As bike share is often provided under public subsidy, greater focus on how to include a broader participation across the income spectrum is needed.

Note

1   GoCard is the SmartCard public transport ticketing used in Brisbane.

References

Alta Bike Share. (2011). *Melbourne Bike Share Survey.* Melbourne: Alta Bike Share.

Australian Bureau of Statistics. (2013). Census 2011. Retrieved from http://www.abs. gov.au/websitedbs/censushome.nsf/home/data?opendocument&navpos=200

Bachand-Marleau, J., Lee, B. H. Y., & El-Geneidy, A. M. (2012). Better understanding of factors influencing likelihood of using shared bicycle systems and frequency of use. *Transportation Research Record: Journal of the Transportation Research Board, 2314,* 66–71. doi:10.3141/2314-09

Buck, D., & Buehler, R. (2011). *Bike lanes and other determinants of Capital Bikeshare trips.* Paper presented at the Transportation Research Board Annual Meeting 2012, Washington, DC. Conference paper retrieved from http://ralphbu.files. wordpress.com/2012/02/buck-buehler-poster-cabi-trb-2012.pdf

Department of Infrastructure and Transport. (2013). *Walking, Riding and Access to Public Transport.* Canberra: Australian Government. Retrieved from https:// infrastructure.gov.au/infrastructure/pab/active_transport/files/active_travel_ discussion.pdf

Doonan, K. (2010). Setting the Transport Scene in SEQ. Retrieved from Brisbane: https://www.planning.org.au/documents/item/2192

Fishman, E. (2014). *Bikeshare: Barriers, facilitators and impacts on car use* (PhD thesis by publication). Queensland University of Technology, Brisbane.

Fishman, E. (2015). Bikeshare: A review of recent literature. *Transport Reviews,* 1–22. doi:10.1080/01441647.2015.1033036

Fishman, E., & Brennan, T. (2010). *Oil vulnerability in Melbourne.* Paper presented at the Australasian Transport Research Forum, Canberra.

Fishman, E., Washington, S., & Haworth, N. (2012). Barriers and facilitators to public bicycle scheme use: A qualitative approach. *Transportation Research Part F-Traffic Psychology and Behaviour, 15*(6), 686–698.

Fishman, E., Washington, S., Haworth, N., & Mazzei, A. (2014). Barriers to bikesharing: An analysis from Melbourne and Brisbane. *Journal of Transport Geography, 41,* 325–337.

Fishman, E., Washington, S., Haworth, N., & Watson, A. (2015). Factors influencing bike share membership: An analysis of Melbourne and Brisbane. *Transportation Research Part A, 71,* 17–30. doi:10.1016/j.tra.2014.10.021

Fuller, D., Gauvin, L., Kestens, Y., Daniel, M., Fournier, M., Morency, P., & Drouin, L. (2011). Use of a new public bicycle share program in Montreal, Canada. *American Journal of Preventive Medicine, 41*(1), 80–83. doi:10.1016/j.amepre.2011.03.002

Institute for Transportation & Development Policy. (2018). The Bikeshare Planning Guide. Retrieved from New York: https://www.itdp.org/publication/the-bike-share-planning-guide/

LDA Consulting. (2012). Capital Bikeshare 2011 Member Survey Report. Retrieved from Washington, DC: https://d21xlh2maitm24.cloudfront.net/wdc/Capital-Bikeshare-SurveyReport-Final.pdf?mtime=20161206135935

LDA Consulting. (2013). 2013 Capital Bikeshare Member Survey Report. Retrieved from Washington, DC: http://capitalbikeshare.com/assets/pdf/CABI-2013SurveyReport.pdf

LDA Consulting. (2017). 2016 Capital Bikeshare Member Survey Report. Retrieved from Washington, DC: https://d21xlh2maitm24.cloudfront.net/wdc/Capital-Bikeshare_2016MemberSurvey_Executive-Summary.pdf?mtime=20170303165533

Lewis, T. (2011). Has London's cycle hire scheme been a capital idea? *Guardian.* Retrieved from http://www.guardian.co.uk/uk/bike-blog/2011/jul/10/boris-bikes-hire-scheme-london?commentpage=all#start-of-comments

Médard de Chardon, C., Caruso, G., & Thomas, I. (2017). Bicycle sharing system 'success' determinants. *Transportation Research Part A: Policy and Practice, 100,* 202–214.

Molina-Garcia, J., Castillo, I., Queralt, A., & Sallis, J. F. (2013). Bicycling to university: Evaluation of a bicycle-sharing program in Spain. *Health Promotion International.* doi:10.1093/heapro/dat045

Pucher, J., Buehler, R., & Seinen, M. (2011). Bicycling renaissance in North America? An update and re-appraisal of cycling trends and policies. *Transportation Research Part A: Policy and Practice, 45*(6), 451–475. doi:10.1016/j.tra.2011.03.001

Pucher, J., Greaves, S., & Garrard, J. (2010). Cycling down under: A comparative analysis of bicycling trends and policies in Sydney and Melbourne. *Journal of Transport Geography, 19*(2), 332–345.

Shaheen, S., Martin, E., Cohen, A. P., & Finson, R. (2012). Public Bikesharing in North America: Early Operator and User Understanding (11-26). Retrieved from San Jose: https://transweb.sjsu.edu/sites/default/files/1029-public-bikesharing-understanding-early-operators-users.pdf

Shaheen, S., Zhang, H., Martin, E., & Guzman, S. (2011). Hangzhou public bicycle: Understanding early adoption and behavioural response to bike sharing in Hangzhou, China. *Transportation Research Record: Journal of the Transportation Research Board, 2247,* 33–41.

Traffix Group. (2012). *Evaluation of Melbourne Bike Share.* Melbourne: Traffix Group, for VicRoads.

Transport for London. (2010). Travel in London Report 3. Retrieved from London: http://www.tfl.gov.uk/assets/downloads/corporate/travel-in-london-report-3.pdf

Transport for London. (2018). Santander Cycles Customer Satisfaction and Usage Survey Casual Users Only: Quarter 2 2017/18. Retrieved from London: http://content.tfl.gov.uk/santander-cycles-casuals-css-q2-2017-18.pdf

Virginia Tech. (2012). Capital Bikeshare Study: A Closer Look at Casual Users and Operation. Retrieved from Arlington: https://ralphbu.files.wordpress.com/2012/01/vt-bike-share-study-final3.pdf

11 Bike Share Catchment and Station Location Planning

Like any other public transport investment, bike share funds are limited, and there is a requirement to maximise the public benefit. Docked bike share programs, in particular, do come at significant upfront capital expenditure and therefore it is prudent to locate docking stations in the areas of the city likely to gain maximum use. It goes without saying that a well-used bike share system offers more benefit to a city than one that attracts few users. This chapter introduces a data-led, Geographic Information System (GIS) method of designing bike share catchments focused on maximising usage. This *Bike Share Propensity Index* is designed to show the variation in the *relative* propensity to use bike share at the highest possible level of spatial detail, across a chosen metropolitan area. It is based on the logistic regression analysis presented in the previous chapter.

11.1 Catchment Design – Developing a Bike Share Propensity Index

A selection of variables have been collected and combined to develop a composite designed to map changing underlying demographics that are predictive of future bike share use. The data that form the basis of the Index relate to known determinants of bike share membership. Whilst these data have been collected from Australian survey respondents, the underlying characteristics of bike share members are similar to earlier work from samples in London (Transport for London, 2014) and the United States (Buck & Buehler, 2011; Buck et al., 2013; LDA Consulting, 2013).

To provide a real-life example, the case of Sydney, Australia will be used to highlight how a *Bike Share Propensity Index* works. Whilst Sydney is used in this example, providing the necessary Census is present, the Index can be applied to any city interested in designing a bike share catchment. The datasets that have been used to act as the basis for the *Bike Share Propensity Index* are drawn from Sydney data collected in the 2011 Australian Census. Similar datasets are available for most OECD countries:

1   Residential population density, measured as *people per hectare*.
2   Employment density, measured as *number of people working per hectare*.

3   Density of young people, measured as *number of people aged 18–34 years per hectare*.

4   City-based employment, measured as the *number of employed people across Sydney with employment destinations within the Sydney-Haymarket-The Rocks SA2*, by residential SA2.[1]

5   Low motor vehicle ownership, measured as the *number of households with one or zero motor vehicles per hectare*.

6   Bicycle use – origin, measured as the *number of workers per hectare who used the bicycle for at least one stage of their trip to work*, by residential SA2.

7   Bicycle use – destination, measured as the *number of workers per hectare who used the bicycle for at least one stage of their trip to work*, by destination SA2.

The seven datasets identified above have been mapped, showing their variation across inner Sydney. It should be noted that these are not the only factors that influence bike share use; however, each of them have been found to be predictors of bike share use in earlier work, described in Chapter 10 (Fishman, Washington, Haworth, & Watson, 2015).

The *Bike Share Propensity Index* shows the variation in the *relative* propensity to use bike share at the highest possible level of detail. There are 2,617 individual geographic areas that make up the *Propensity Index* map for Sydney. Geographic areas that rank in the bottom quintile (Q1) receive a score of 0.2 for that attribute, whilst those in the top quintile receive 1.0, as shown in Table 11.1. The mapped values are aggregates of the seven attributes' scores.

It should be noted that not all factors influencing bike share use have been included in the *Bike Share Propensity Index*. The factors known to be omitted from the Index include hotel room density, public transport hubs, major sporting and shopping destinations, convention centres, entertainment venues and bike infrastructure.[2] These factors can be used to inform precise siting of docking stations. In other cities, geographic data on these variables may exist and could be used to enhance the Index further.

Table 11.1 Ranking system for geographic areas and Index categories

Geographic areas ranked lowest to highest	Quintile	Index score
0–524	1	0.2
425–1,047	2	0.4
1,048–11,570	3	0.6
1,571–2,093	4	0.8
2,094–2,617	5	1.0

11.1.1 Sydney's Bike Share Catchment

In order to rationalise the size of a potential bike share catchment area for Sydney, areas displaying relatively high propensity to use bike share have been distilled. In this way, docking stations are only placed in parts of Sydney that have a combination of characteristics predictive of bike share use (e.g., relatively low motor vehicle ownership, relatively high current riding levels and high numbers of people aged 18–34).

Figure 11.1 illustrates the outcome of the *Bike Share Propensity Index*, with darker regions indicating higher likelihood of bike share use. It is important to note Figure 11.1 shows *relative* propensity for bike share use. Thus, the darkest regions are only indicative of higher bike share propensity relative to the other areas of Sydney. No comparison can be made with other cities. For those familiar with Sydney, the areas displaying the strongest attributes for bike share include Surry Hills, Darlinghurst, Ultimo, Erskineville and the area around the University of Sydney.

The Sydney CBD (downtown) is not among the highest rated areas in Figure 11.1. The reason for this is not necessarily a lack of latent bike share demand. It is more likely to be that the variables that make up the Index are skewed towards *residential* location factors rather than *employment* based factors. It may therefore by necessary to apply a weighting factor of around 1.5–2, for the employment factors (e.g., job density), to account for this.

11.1.2 Phasing Bike Share Implementation

Due to financial and logistical constraints, it is often necessary to phase bike share in multiple stages. To continue with the example of Sydney, using the propensity index shown in Figure 11.1, 632 docking stations (capable of holding ten bicycles each) and a fleet of 3,160 bicycles has been recommended. A docking station density of 9 per km^2 has been used, which is based on best practice design principles (City & County of Honolulu, 2014; Institute for Transportation & Development Policy, 2013, 2018a; NACTO, 2016). This provides the best balance between maximising the coverage of the program and ensuring users are never more than a five-minute walk between docking stations. This is important when docking stations become 100% full or empty, and a user must travel to the next closest station (NACTO, 2016).

The Phase 1 catchment and docking station locations are shown in Figure 11.2. Conceptually, the objective underpinning the docking station catchment shown in the figure has been to offer bike share in the locations showing the strongest prospective use. However, it is important to note that the docking station locations shown in the figure have been chosen for *illustrative purposes* and precise locations will need refinement should Sydney choose to establish a bike share program. A good example is the University of Sydney, which did not show up high on the Propensity

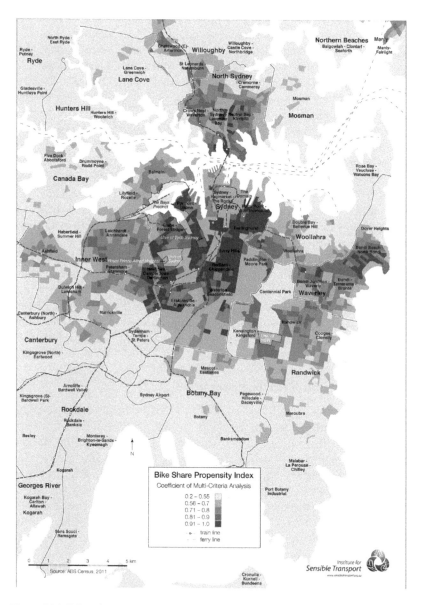

Figure 11.1 Bike Share Propensity Index map for Sydney.
Source: Fishman, Schmitt, & Baker (2016).

Index, due to limited residential population, yet is very likely to be a popular location to start and finish bike share trips in a future Sydney bike share program. Centrally located university campuses are likely to be a bike share hotspot, due to a combination of the density of people, their age (young adults) and limited car parking and ownership levels.

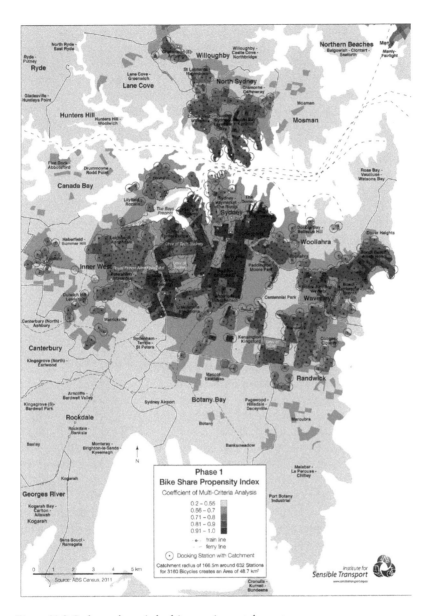

Figure 11.2 Sydney phase 1 docking station catchment.
Source: Fishman et al. (2016).

Strategically, the catchment offers the best balance between system cost and usability. In addition to offering an attractive alternative to short car trips in inner city Sydney, it enhances first/last mile connectivity with the public transport system. The analysis has found that North Sydney demonstrates relatively high bike share propensity, and it is likely that docking stations on both sides of the Sydney Harbour Bridge would be popular with commuters, as well as recreational riders, including high numbers of tourists.

As a validation exercise, *GoGet* car share pods in Sydney have been mapped, and this has been compared to the proposed Phase 1 docking station catchment and shows a high degree of overlap. This is considered important given that it is very likely that the factors that influence membership of car share are likely to be similar to bike share.

A second phase was recommended and proposes an additional 2,195 bicycles (see Figure 11.3), to assist in making bike share a viable option for a larger proportion of the Sydney population. The proposed catchment for Phase 2 continues to be informed by the results of the *Bike Share Propensity Index*, in which docking station deployment is based on higher levels of expected bike share use. The Phase 2 catchment includes 439 docking stations and uses the same docking station density as for Phase 1 (9 per km^2). The rollout of Phase 2 should only be determined once a detailed evaluation of the Phase 1 bike share program has been completed between 1 and 2 years after Phase 1 is implemented.

Phase 2 could be further informed from customer and potential customer feedback following Phase 1. For instance, customers may request docking stations in particular locations that fall outside the high-ranking areas of the Propensity Index. 'Demand-responsive' implementation practice is well established within North American bike share planning. This often includes the development of a digital platform in which members of the public are able to submit their preferred locations for future docking stations, or comment/vote on other people's contribution. The results can then be used within standard GIS software to make modifications to future system expansion plans.

The costs for implementing Phases 1 and 2, with 5,355 bicycles, at an average unit cost of $A8,000 per bike comes to around $A43 million. This is a substantial cost. It is, however, useful to place these costs within the context of public transport infrastructure improvements. The costs associated with implementing the proposed system should be seen as an investment in the public transport network. When the costs of implementing Phases 1 and 2 of the proposed system are seen in the context of public transport costs, they appear modest by comparison. For instance, a typical tram in Melbourne costs around $A5,000,000–$A8,000,000 and a 12.5 m Volgren bus costs ~$A500,000–$A750,000.

It is of course important to mention that these results arose from an official bike share feasibility study commissioned by several Sydney inner city councils. The study was completed in 2016 and since that time, dockless bike share has emerged that offer cities another way of providing large scale bike share without the upfront costs. As identified earlier in this book, a range of dockless bike share firms established operations in 2017, but by the end of 2018, only one of the original operators remain (Mobike), whilst another (LIME) offering dockless, electric assist bike share began operating in 2018, and now has 2,000 bikes. This demonstrates the current willingness of the private sector to risk their capital, in

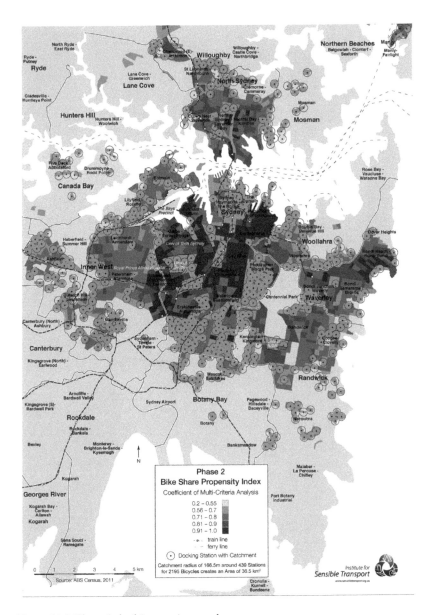

Figure 11.3 Phase 2 docking station catchment.
Source: Fishman et al. (2016).

the hope that the revenue that is returned to them in the form of user fees
covers these establishment and on-going operational costs. As mentioned
earlier, there is no guarantee that this private sector financed bike share
model will persistent into the future. Government should be prepared
for the possibility that the commercial sector may withdraw their service

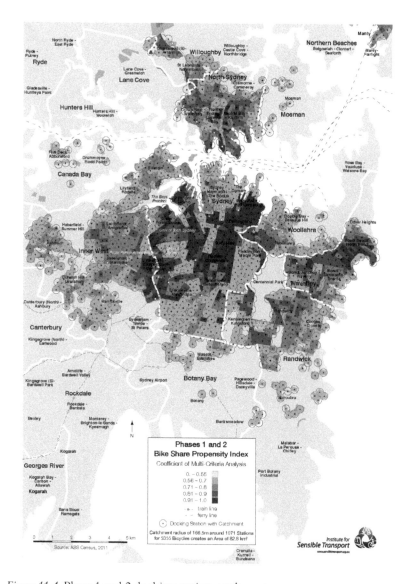

Figure 11.4 Phase 1 and 2 docking station catchment.
Source: Fishman et al. (2016).

should costs continue to be higher than revenue. As mentioned earlier, it is important for governments to weigh carefully the relative costs and benefits before electing whether to offer a docked or dockless system. City governments need to determine which model holds the best prospects of helping to meet their wider strategic objectives and dictate the terms under which bike share operates in their city (Figure 11.4).

11.2 Docking Station Placement

The previous section showed how the Propensity Index can be a useful method of using city-level data to determine the best docking station catchment at the macroscopic level. This section narrows the focus by looking at the 'scale of the street' to determine the siting of individual docking stations.

The location of docking stations plays a critical role in the performance of bike share. One of the best awareness raising and marketing tools for bike share is simply seeing the bikes, and this is best achieved through siting in high-exposure locations. Docking stations that are positioned in obscure locations are unlikely to be well used, limiting the overall effectiveness of the bike share network. Moreover, docking stations placed in neighbourhoods with few underlying demographic and population characteristics favourable to bike share also limit the performance of the bike share system.

Bike share docking stations can be thought of like 'little bus stops'; those located in areas that maximise convenience and awareness are more likely to attract the greatest ridership. Research from Minneapolis and New York City has found that businesses with docking stations nearby show increased economic activity, especially for restaurants (NACTO, 2016). Similarly, in Washington, D.C., Buehler and Hamre (2015) found significant economic benefit to shops located close to docking stations. In other studies, docking stations that replace kerbside car parking were found to substantially increase commercial return to local businesses, as one car space provides sufficient room for ten bike share slots (NACTO, 2016).

Docking stations can either be fixed to the ground (e.g., Paris, London, Brisbane) or modular (e.g., Melbourne, New York City, Washington, D.C.). Module systems require no excavation or other intense infrastructure installation, and it is for this reason that they are now the prevailing trend in docking station provision. Their easier installation also allows for a more flexible system, capable of re-locations following system performance evaluations or for special events. This section refers to the modular type of docking station.

11.2.1 Placement Principles

The overarching principle that ought to govern the position of docking stations is the location's attributes for overall system usage. Whilst maximising system usage should be the overall goal when selecting individual sites for docking stations, there are several sub-principles that should be considered, as outlined below.

- Support for integration with public transport.
- Highly visible: Attracts users and sponsorship interest.
- Located near major trip attractors: Large retail, universities, office or sporting/arts venues.

- Able to be accessed by service vehicles.
- Support from local council and other stakeholders.
- Maximise system access and equity of usage, especially low-income groups.
- Supported by bicycle infrastructure: Docking stations along high quality bicycle infrastructure have higher usage levels (Buck & Buehler, 2011).
- Supporting a contiguous network, in which docking stations are within a short (less than 5 minutes) walk to the next closest docking station.
- Exposure to sufficient sunlight if relying on solar power or access to electrical network if shading is unavoidable.
- Does not provide significant disruptions to pedestrian traffic.
- Does not impede emergency or public transport vehicles.

11.2.2 Public Consultation

Public consultation is an important component in the final positioning of docking stations. It is common, particularly for North American bike share programs, to hold a range of digital and face-to-face community engagement events to help align docking station locations with public demand. Digital platforms provide an easy way for the public to suggest a location for a docking station and for others to leave a comment of support (or otherwise). As shown earlier, the results can then be exported into GIS software to allow bike share planners to further refine the siting of docking stations.

For face-to-face community engagement sessions, it can be useful to provide events focused on a particular neighbourhood and provide a box with three potential locations and ask participants to select the one that makes the most sense to them. The results of this activity can then be used to further refine the precise location of stations. In areas that are culturally and linguistically diverse, it may be helpful to have interpreters, to ensure all the key cultural groups are included in the consultation process.

11.2.3 Different Types of Locations

Broadly speaking, docking station locations can be divided into the following typologies:

1 On-street
2 On-footpath
3 Open spaces: Parks and pedestrianised areas.

11.2.4 Density

Best practice station densities allow users to walk from one station to another within 5 minutes, which equates to ~300–400 m (NACTO, 2015). This results in a docking station density of around 11 per km^2 (Institute for Transportation & Development Policy, 2018b). As previously outlined, this is important particularly in instances when a rider seeking to return a bike encounters a station that is 100% full. They must ride to the next station (which is often in the opposite direction to their final destination). Minimum station densities help to ensure they do not have to divert too far from their intended destination. Similarly, when seeking to begin a ride, a docking station that is 100% empty will require the user to walk to the next closest docking station. Ensuring this walk is less than 5 minutes will help to mitigate user frustration with the inevitable temporary imbalances of bicycles across the network and reduce travel time reliability issues.

The principle of keeping docking stations within a 5-minute walk from one another was used in the previous section outlining the proposed catchment of a future Sydney bike share system. This resulted in a density of nine docking stations per km^2.

11.2.5 Docking Station Size

Docking stations typically house a minimum of ten bicycles each but can be expanded to include hundreds of bicycles if demand and space allows. Figure 11.5 provides an illustration of the space requirements for different docking station configurations. The dimensions shown in Figure 11.5 have been based on the hardware used in Melbourne and should be viewed as approximate. Most cities choose to use a variety of the four key configuration types (angled, standard, double-sided and back-to-back), based on the characteristics of location in which they are to be sited. Whilst less common, it is also possible to have curved and right-angled docking stations.

11.2.6 Docking Station Types

11.2.6.1 Street Stations

It is very common for docking stations to be located on the street itself. In areas of high pedestrian volume, street stations are preferred, in order to minimise any disruption to pedestrian flow. Space previously used as kerb-side motor vehicle parking is often used for street stations, and an example from Brisbane is shown in Figure 11.6.

When bicycles are parked at 90 degrees, the docking stations are still narrower than a parked car. Stations can have bicycles orientated to be removed towards the street (as shown in Figure 11.6) or the opposite way, so they back out onto the footpath, should space requirements allow. When it is desirable to remove roadway width (e.g., to calm traffic/increase safety), having bicycles back out onto the footpath may be appropriate, as it requires additional space.

It has been argued that street stations support city objectives related to traffic calming, safety and sustainability, as it helps to reallocate road

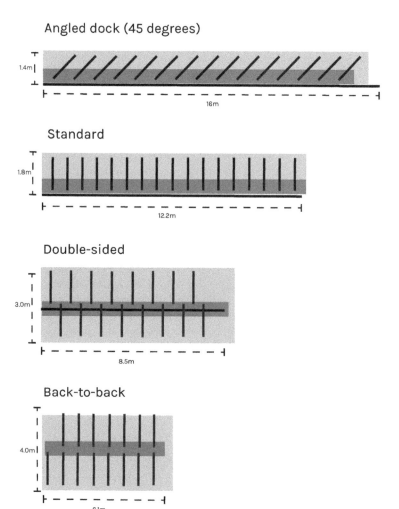

Figure 11.5 Docking station space requirements.
Source: Based on work by NACTO (2016).

space to sustainable mobility, without removing space currently used by pedestrians (NACTO, 2016). In relation to safety, street stations are now approved by the New York City Department of Transportation as a method of increasing visibility of pedestrians at intersections; however, it is important any additional kiosk infrastructure (e.g., map boards) do not obstruct the view of pedestrians from passing motorists (NACTO, 2016).

On street stations can even be used to create protected bicycle lanes, as shown in Figure 11.7 from Austin, Texas. This solution is particularly elegant when one considers that docking stations located on bicycle routes are

Figure 11.6 A station street in Brisbane's CityCycle program.
Source: Institute for Sensible Transport.

Figure 11.7 Docking station providing protection for bike lane, Austin, TX.
Source: NACTO (2016).

used significantly more than those disconnected from bike lanes (Buck & Buehler, 2011). This type of configuration is not unique to Austin and is used in the design of the *Citi Bike* and *Capital Bikeshare* systems.

Readers seeking more information regarding docking station siting are encouraged to read NACTO's 2016 *Bike Share: Station Siting Guide.*

11.2.6.2 Footpath Stations

In locations with insufficient kerbside road space to accommodate a docking station, it is possible to use footpaths (as shown in Figure 11.8), providing it does not impede the flow of pedestrians. A minimum of 2 m clearance from the back of the bike is required to ensure the removal of a bike does not create issues for pedestrians and potentially DDA compliance complications.

Figure 11.8 shows the docking station positioned against the kerb, but it is also possible to locate docking stations on pavements against the property line, or other places on the footpath provided it does not create access issues. Footpath stations against kerbs with car parking need to provide additional clearance to allow car doors to open.

One configuration that blends aspects of *on street* and *on footpath* siting is the 'Bike Share Bulb Out', in which a footpath extension provides sufficient space for a docking station. This is particularly applicable to sites with high pedestrian volumes, such as outside train stations or popular shopping streets. This type of design is shown in Figure 11.9.

11.2.6.3 Park/Plaza Stations

Parks and other pedestrianised areas are often used for docking stations and can help to activate parks and other areas. For docking stations in

Figure 11.8 Footpath station, Melbourne.
Source: Institute for Sensible Transport.

Figure 11.9 Bulb Out docking station, Arlington, Virginia.
Source: NACTO (2016).

parks, it is important that safety and security issues are considered, especially late at night. In many US cities, stations at the entrance to parks and plazas are some of the most used across the system.

In general, it is better to place docking stations on the periphery rather than the centre of a park, so they can be more easily used by people whether they are using the park or not Figure 11.10 illustrates one of the *CityCycle* docking stations outside the Brisbane Botanic Gardens.

Docking stations have also been used as part of reactivation initiatives, as the people it brings to a site can have important economic impacts on cafes and restaurants (NACTO, 2016). Docking stations can even be used as part of small street closures.

Finally, in a number of US cities, bike share docking stations have been successfully integrated into at grade locations previously used as car parks. It is important these locations are highly visible, as they may otherwise go unnoticed by the public. The emergence of driverless cars and the opportunities this creates for shared mobility is also widely predicted to reduce the need for car parks and open possibilities for this space to be repurposed (Fragnant & Kockelman, 2018; Fishman, 2016b; Navigant Research, 2016; PwC, 2015). Bike share is one obvious use among many potential options. With between 15% and 30% of urban area dedicated to car parks (Shoup, 2005), it is difficult to overstate the significance of this pivotal moment in the history of urban transport to repurpose space formerly dedicated to cars towards more people-orientated purposes.

Figure 11.10 CityCycle docking stations outside Brisbane Botanical Gardens.
Source: Institute for Sensible Transport.

11.3 Integrating Bike Share and Public Transport

A seamless integration of bike share with public transport can make up for
the weaknesses of both modes and increase the convenience and efficiency
of sustainable mobility (Fishman & Hart, 2010; Martens, 2004; Pucher &
Buehler, 2008). Combining cycling and public transport is critical to successful *integrated* transport planning (Givoni & Banister, 2010).

This section is intended to outline mechanisms through which the bike
share and public transport systems can be designed to offer a seamless
connection. Indeed, some commentators have noted that bike share *is*
public transport. Eric Britton, an American transport commentator, who
is an established resident of Paris noted soon after the launch of the *Velib*
system in 2007 that the program should be thought of as 20,000 *little
buses*. Similarly, Paul DeMaio, an experienced bike share planner based
in the Washington, D.C. area has argued that bike share docking stations
should be thought of as little bus stops, meaning they need to be placed
in prominent locations, to improve awareness and usability (as discussed
above).

Bike share systems are in some cases funded out of public transport budgets
and this would appear to be a clear acknowledgement that bike share is seen
by some agencies as a legitimate component of the wider public transport
service.

Research from Australia, North America and Great Britain shows that bike share users have a strong revealed preference for integrating bike share and public transport (Lansell, 2011; LDA Consulting, 2013; Transport for London, 2014). Analysis of bike share docking station activity show significantly higher intensity (number of bicycles taken and returned) at docking stations located near public transport hubs. Indeed, the spikes in usage coinciding with peak public transport demand (Lansell, 2011). Surveys of North American bike share users confirm frequent trip patterns that combine bike share use with public transport (Shaheen, Martin, Cohen, & Finson, 2012), with London bike share users reporting similar habits (Transport for London, 2014).

Does bike share compete with or complement public transport use? Scholars at the National Center for Smart Growth Research and Education in Maryland conducted a study attempting to answer this question. Analysing ridership data from *Capital Bikeshare* and *Metrorail* in the Washington, D.C. region, as well as a range of population, demographic and density data, the researchers found that *Capital Bikeshare* docking stations located near Metrorail stations had significantly higher ridership. Their statistical analysis found that a 10% increase in *Capital Bikeshare* trips would increase transit ridership by 2.8%. This study allowed the authors to conclude that rather than competing with rail, bike share in effect increased overall transit ridership (Ma, Liu, & Erdoğan, 2015).

This trend of using bike share in combination with public transport has come about largely in the absence of widespread strategic coordination between those managing the public transport network and those responsible for the bike share system. Whilst there are welcome instances in which policies have been developed intended to orchestrate this modal integration, for the most part, it is simply a case of users identifying the inevitable weaknesses in the coverage of the public transport network and using bike share to bridge the gap, in order to improve the door-to-door travel time competitiveness. A clear demonstration of this effect in action can be seen from an examination of bike share data from Melbourne (Fishman, Washington, Haworth, & Mazzei, 2014). Figure 11.11 highlights the relationship between bike share docking stations for one month's use of the *Melbourne Bike Share* program (November 2012). The bike symbols in Figure 11.11 represent docking stations. Any two stations recording more than 50 trips between them have been represented with a line. The width of the line corresponds with the number of trips occurring between the two stations (see Legend). Public transit accessibility has also been included, using the established Public Transport Accessibility Levels (PTAL) methodology (Transport for London, 2010). The PTAL is divided into six levels (1–6), with 6 representing high accessibility (shown as dark areas in Figure 11.11).[3]

Many of the strongest trip patterns shown in Figure 11.11 occur between stations located in areas of relatively weak public transport accessibility. This may be explained by the journey time competitiveness of bike share in these areas. Travel time is a key determinant of mode choice (Sener,

Figure 11.11 Major relationships between docking stations, Melbourne Bike
          Share, November 2012.
Source: Fishman et al. (2014).

Eluru, & Bhat, 2009), and it is likely the increased utility afforded by bike
share in areas of lower public transport accessibility explains the relationship illustrated in Figure 11.11. This is consistent with research conducted
in Helsinki that found the greatest travel time savings associated with bike
share and public transport can be found in areas in which the public transport network is less developed (Jäppinen, Toivonen, & Salonen, 2013).

11.3.1 Physical Integration

As highlighted earlier, bike share is well recognised for its ability to provide
a first/last mile solution to public transport (Shaheen, Guzman, & Zhang,
2010). Figure 11.12 demonstrates how connecting train stations with neighbourhoods through a cohesive networks of bike lanes/paths can increase

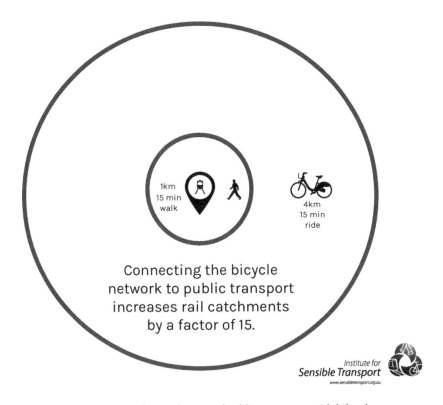

Figure 11.12 Increasing the catchment of public transport with bike share.
Source: Hudson (1982).

the catchment area of public transport by a factor of 15 (Hudson, 1982). Ensuring bike share programs are able to support people's preference for multi-modal integration through the positioning of docking stations that can allow bike share to be a feeder mode to transit, in combination with bicycle route infrastructure is essential to their successful integration.

Box 11.1 Integrating Citi Bike with New York City's transit system

Citi Bike supports the public transport system by providing a last mile option for getting to/from a public transport stop. Even within the relatively dense network of the NYC rail system there are still areas that are beyond a comfortable walk to the nearest

(Continued)

train station. Almost three-quarters of all *Citi Bike* docking stations are within a five minute walk of a subway station (Kaufman, Gordon-Koven, Levenson, & Moss, 2015). This helps to reduce door-to-door travel time when combining *Citi Bike* and public transport. On average there are two *Citi Bike* docking stations for every subway station.

An analysis of the *Citi Bike* docking stations with the highest number of trips shows that they are typically directly outside transport hubs (Kaufman et al., 2015), suggesting that users are combining public transport with *Citi Bike*. There are no known arrangements to allow *Citi Bike* access via public transport smartcard at the present time.

Many train stations experience car parking capacity issues. Research conducted in Melbourne, Australia found between 12% and 25% of cars parked at train stations originate from within one kilometre (Fishman & von Wyss, 2016), suggesting some low hanging fruit when seeking to shift to more efficient transport. Bike share could serve as an efficient and convenient substitute for short car trips to train stations.

Recommendations for enhancing the physical integration of bike share public transport include:

1   Develop high-quality bicycle routes leading to train stations, preferably protected bicycle lanes/paths. Using the concept shown in Figure 11.1 can be a helpful guide to route planning, to ensure the catchment area of the public transport system is maximised.
2   Locate docking stations within 250 m of trip origin (e.g., home address). The likelihood of being a bike share member is substantially higher for those living within 250 m of a docking station (Fishman et al., 2015; Fuller et al., 2011). It is impractical to be able to locate docking stations within 250 m of every residential address and therefore, all other factors being equal, areas of relatively high density should be prioritised. Placement of bike share docking stations in strategic locations within a 2 km radius of train stations as 'origin' bike share stations is recommended.
3   Ensure docking stations have the capacity to serve train stations. With relatively large numbers of people using bike share to access train stations, sufficient capacity is necessary to dock bikes within a short walk of public transport hubs. One technology option that could be helpful in this regard are so-called 'hybrid' systems in which bicycles that exceed the capacity of a docking station can be locked to itself, in a 'virtual docking station', next to a physical docking station. GPS-enabled bikes allow the rider to dock their bike within a designated, geofenced zone. This function may be helpful in high demand areas

that experience substantial volumes of drop offs in short time periods (e.g., around train stations).

4 Constrain car parking options around train stations. People to not make bike share decisions in isolation from other transport modes. When a train station has high levels of car parking, this reduces the attractiveness of using more space efficient modes like bike share. Therefore, all other factors being equal, a station that has a car park that frequently reaches 100% capacity early in the AM peak will have higher levels of bike share use. Bike share should be seen as an opportunity to bring rail customers to the station without the space demands inherent in parking motor vehicles.

11.3.2 Digital Integration

The degree to which bike share integrates with public transport from a digital technology perspective is becoming increasingly important. 'Mobile first' is becoming a mantra within bike share firms that are seeking to align their offer with market preferences. The ubiquity of the smartphone has created the foundation for a wide variety of mobile applications (Apps) focused on transport information. Many of these Apps share a common goal of enhancing transport mode decision-making (Fishman, 2016b). Utilising GPS capabilities and API feeds from public transport providers, these Apps allow users to receive detailed, real time public transport information. Some Apps are even able to provide detailed, multimodal journey options, including estimated arrival time and price.

An emerging trend in international bike share practice is to integrate bike share within the city's existing public transport system. Over the last few years, a number of cities have moved to a *smartphone-as-the-ticket* platform for paying for public transport. This paves the way for an *access all modes* smartphone application that allows a user to seamlessly integrate multiple modes of transport via one's smartphone application or card (RFID or NFC).[4]

One company that aggregates disparate transport information into one App is the Daimler owned *Moovel*. Moovel lists the available modes between an origin and destination, and shows estimated cost and journey time for each mode. To do this, *Moovel* gathers information from more than 300 transport operators and offers a streamlined payment process.

A standardised open data format was created for bike share in 2015 to assist with back end app integration. Imaginatively titled 'General Bikeshare Feed Specification' (GBFS), it has been adopted by the North American Bikeshare Association and key industry partners. The GBFS makes data feeds publicly available online in a uniform format so that map and transport-based Apps can integrate the data into their platforms. Bike share customers can then use these Apps to find out about station locations, bicycle and dock availability, and pricing information.[5]

When cities are developing contracts with bike share suppliers and operators, it is important to include a requirement that they have an open data feed in GBFS format. Requiring the provider to have systems in place to capture GBFS data and to release a real-time GBFS feed will eliminate the risk of having to develop potentially expensive bespoke (single-mode) Apps.

One of the most consistent preferences expressed by current and potential bike share users is the ability to use an existing public transport smartcard to access bike share (Fishman, 2014, 2016a). This lowers the barriers to entry or the 'friction' that is often involved in signing up to something new (Fishman, Washington, & Haworth, 2012). By allowing those who have a credit-card-linked public transport smartcard to also use this card to swipe out a bicycle is another step closer to the seamless integration of bike share with public transport. In essence, bike share becomes a new mode within the wider public transport system. Whilst it is important not to ignore the complexities this integration can involve (e.g., multi-jurisdictional collaboration, insurance, easily comprehensible fee structures), the benefits are significant in terms of enhanced transport convenience and simplicity.

One of the biggest changes many cities will experience with the way they access their public transport system over coming years will be the introduction of smartphone ticketing. Portland, Chicago and a number of other cities have already launched programs in which people use their smartphone to pay and access public transport, eliminating the need for a dedicated public transport smartcard.

The integration of bike share and public transport offers an important opportunity to add a new mode to the existing public transport system. Visitors and residents will benefit from the finer grain network made possible by a bike share program. In addition to providing safe routes to train stations, a bike share scheme will need to offer docking stations within the 1–3 km (5–15 minutes ride) catchment of train stations. A large number of docking stations (or bike parking corrals for dockless systems) will need to be located around some train stations to receive the peak hour flows of commuters. This may require overflow corrals (as is the case in some parts of the Washington, D.C. bike share program) and/or require rebalancing teams to place bikes in areas with empty docking stations. To further reduce the impact of peak demand flows, GPS and other mobile technology combined with pricing incentives (discounts) may be used to encourage users to travel against the prevailing flow of bikes, to lessen the redistribution task of the bike share operator.

Notes

1 An SA2 is a Statistical Area Level 2, as defined by the Australian Bureau of Statistics. See http://www.abs.gov.au/ausstats/abs@.nsf/Latestproducts/88F6A0EDEB8879C0CA257801000C64D9.

2 Though bike infrastructure does not form part of the Propensity Index, *trips by bike* does, and this is considered a reliable proxy.
3 PTALs are a measure of the accessibility of a point to the public transport network, taking into account walk access time, service availability and frequency.
4 RFID: Radio Frequency Identification. NCF: Near Field Communication. Both technologies are used in public transport smart card ticketing.
5 https://github.com/NABSA/gbfs.

References

Buck, D., & Buehler, R. (2011). *Bike lanes and other determinants of Capital Bikeshare trips.* Paper presented at the Transportation Research Board Annual Meeting 2012, Washington, DC. Conference paper retrieved from http://ralphbu.files. wordpress.com/2012/02/buck-buehler-poster-cabi-trb-2012.pdf

Buck, D., Buehler, R., Happ, P., Rawls, B., Chung, P. P., & Borecki, N. (2013). Are bikeshare users different from regular cyclists? *Transportation Research Record: Journal of the Transportation Research Board, 2387*(1), 112–119.

Buehler, R., & Hamre, A. (2015). Business and bikeshare user perceptions of the economic benefits of capital bikeshare. In *Vol. 2520. Transportation Research Record* (pp. 100–111). Washington, D.C.: National Research Council.

City & County of Honolulu. (2014). Honolulu Bikeshare Organizational Study. Retrieved from Honolulu: http://www.oahumpo.org/wp-content/uploads/2013/02/HonoluluBikeshareOrgStudyJune2014.pdf

Fagnant, D. J., & Kockelman, K. (2015). Preparing a nation for autonomous vehicles: opportunities, barriers and policy recommendations. *Transportation Research Part A: Policy and Practice, 77*, 167–181.

Fishman, E. (2014). *Bikeshare: Barriers, facilitators and impacts on car use.* (PhD thesis by publication). Queensland University of Technology, Brisbane.

Fishman, E. (2016a). Bike Share Options for Adelaide. Retrieved from Melbourne: https://sensibletransport.org.au/wp-content/uploads/2016/02/Bike-share-Options-for-Adelaide-Stage-3-Report-1.04.16DB_LR.pdf

Fishman, E. (2016b). Emerging Transport Technologies: Assessing Impacts and Implications for the City of Melbourne. Retrieved from Melbourne: http://sensibletransport.org.au/project/test-project-1/

Fishman, E., & Hart, P. (2010). A Technical Evaluation of Bicycle Carriage on Victorian Trains and Coaches. Retrieved from Melbourne: https://sensibletransport.org.au/wp-content/uploads/2016/06/Integrating-Cycling-and-Public-Transport-in-Victoria.pdf

Fishman, E., Schmitt, L., & Baker, L. (2016). Sydney Bike Share Feasibility Study: Operational Recommendations. Retrieved from https://sensibletransport.org.au/project/sydney-bike-share-feasibility-study/

Fishman, E., & von Wyss, M. (2016). Car Parking at Train Stations: A Spatial Analysis of Registration Postcode of Cars Parked at Essendon and Moonee Ponds Train Stations.

Fishman, E., Washington, S., & Haworth, N. (2012). Barriers and facilitators to public bicycle scheme use: A qualitative approach. *Transportation Research Part F-Traffic Psychology and Behaviour, 15*(6), 686–698.

Fishman, E., Washington, S., Haworth, N., & Mazzei, A. (2014). Barriers to bikesharing: an analysis from Melbourne and Brisbane. *Journal of Transport Geography, 41*, 325–337.

Fishman, E., Washington, S., Haworth, N., & Watson, A. (2015). Factors influencing bike share membership: An analysis of Melbourne and Brisbane. *Transportation Research Part A, 71,* 17–30. doi:10.1016/j.tra.2014.10.021

Fragnant, D. J., & Kockelman, K. (2018). Dynamic ride-sharing and fleet sizing for a system of shared autonomous vehicles in Austin, Texas. *Transportation, 45*(1), 143–158. https://link.springer.com/article/10.1007/s11116-016-9729-z

Fuller, D., Gauvin, L., Kestens, Y., Daniel, M., Fournier, M., Morency, P., & Drouin, L. (2011). Use of a new public bicycle share program in Montreal, Canada. *American Journal of Preventive Medicine, 41*(1), 80–83. doi:10.1016/j.amepre.2011.03.002

Givoni, M., & Banister, D. (2010). *Integrated Transport From Policy to Practice.* Hoboken, NJ: Taylor & Francis.

Hudson, M. (1982). *Bicycle Planning: Policy and Practice.* London: Architectural Press.

Institute for Transportation & Development Policy. (2013). The Bike-sharing Planning Guide. Retrieved from New York: https://www.itdp.org/the-bike-share-planning-guide-2/

Institute for Transportation & Development Policy. (2018a). The Bikeshare Planning Guide. Retrieved from New York: https://www.itdp.org/publication/the-bike-share-planning-guide/

Institute for Transportation & Development Policy. (2018b). Bikeshare System Information & Performance Metrics. Retrieved from http://bikeshare.itdp.org/wp-content/uploads/2018/06/BIKESHARE_SystemInfoPerformance.pdf

Jäppinen, S., Toivonen, T., & Salonen, M. (2013). Modelling the potential effect of shared bicycles on public transport travel times in Greater Helsinki: An open data approach. *Applied Geography, 43,* 13–24.

Kaufman, S. M., Gordon-Koven, L., Levenson, N., & Moss, M. L. (2015). Citi Bike: The First Two Years. Retrieved from New York: http://wagner.nyu.edu/rudincenter/wp-content/uploads/2015/06/Citi_Bike_First_Two_Years_RudinCenter.pdf

Lansell, K. (2011). *Melbourne bike share and public transport integration* (Master of Urban Planning Minor thesis). University of Melbourne, Melbourne.

LDA Consulting. (2013). 2013 Capital Bikeshare Member Survey Report. Retrieved from Washington, DC: http://capitalbikeshare.com/assets/pdf/CABI-2013SurveyReport.pdf

Ma, T., Liu, C., & Erdoğan, S. (2015). Bicycle sharing and public transit: Does capital bikeshare affect metrorail ridership in Washington, D.C.? In *Vol. 2534. Transportation Research Record* (pp. 1–9). National Research Council.

Martens, K. (2004). The bicycle as a feedering mode: Experiences from three European countries. *Transportation Research Part D: Transport and Environment, 9*(4), 281–294. doi:10.1016/j.trd.2004.02.005

NACTO. (2015). Walkable Station Spacing is Key to Successful Equitable Bike Share. Retrieved from New York: https://nacto.org/wp-content/uploads/2015/09/NACTO_Walkable-Station-Spacing-Is-Key-For-Bike-Share_Sc.pdf

NACTO. (2016). Bike Share: Station Siting Guide. Retrieved from http://nacto.org/2016/04/21/nacto-releases-new-guidance-bike-share-station-placement/

Navigant Research. (2016). Connectivity, Autonomous Technology, On-demand Mobility, and Vehicle Electrification Will Transform Global Passenger Transportation [Press release]. Retrieved from https://www.navigantresearch.com/newsroom/84520

Pucher, J., & Buehler, R. (2008). Making cycling irresistible: Lessons from the Netherlands, Denmark and Germany. *Transport Reviews, 28*(4), 495–528.

PwC. (2015). Connected Car Study 2015: Racing Ahead with Autonomous Cars and Digital Innovation. Retrieved from Germany: http://www.strategyand. pwc.com/media/file/Connected-Car-Study-2015.pdf

Sener, I. N., Eluru, N., & Bhat, C. R. (2009). An analysis of bicycle route choice preferences in Texas, US. *Transportation, 36*(5), 511–539. doi:10.1007/s11116-009-9201-4

Shaheen, S., Guzman, S., & Zhang, H. (2010). Bikesharing in Europe, the Americas, and Asia. *Transportation Research Record: Journal of the Transportation Research Board, 2143*, 159–167. doi:10.3141/2143-20

Shaheen, S., Martin, E., Cohen, A. P., & Finson, R. (2012). Public Bikesharing in North America: Early Operator and User Understanding (11-26). Retrieved from San Jose: https://transweb.sjsu.edu/sites/default/files/1029-public-bikesharing-understanding-early-operators-users.pdf

Shoup, D. (2005). *The High Cost of Free Parking*. Chicago, IL: Planners Press.

Transport for London. (2010). Measuring Public Transport Accessibility Levels. Retrieved from London: http://data.london.gov.uk/documents/PTAL-methodology.pdf

Transport for London. (2014). Barclays Cycle Hire customer satisfaction and usage survey: Members Only. Retrieved from London: http://www.tfl.gov.uk/cdn/static/cms/documents/barclays-cycle-hire-css-and-usage-members-q3-2013-14.pdf

12 Getting the Most Out of Bike Share

Designing a User-Orientated System – Summary of Key Factors

A number of best practice principles can be drawn from the literature covered in this book. *Safety, convenience* and *spontaneity* are the key principles upon which current and prospective bike share planners should focus, in their efforts to optimise usage and overall system effectiveness. These principles and their sub-components are identified in Figure 12.1.

The best practice principles identified in Figure 12.1 have been developed through an analysis of cities with successful bike share programs, as well as those cities that have hosted under-performing schemes. One overarching consideration that may be helpful for cities beginning the process of examining a future bike share program is consideration of the *value proposition* offered by the program. Just as public transport planners have been encouraged to 'think like a passenger', it is helpful for bike share planners to 'think like a rider'. What *compelling value proposition* do people

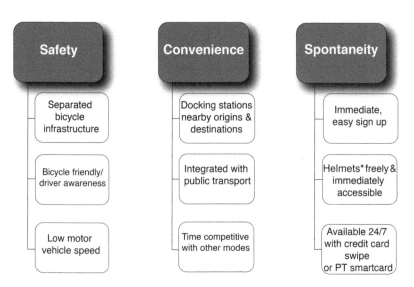

Figure 12.1 Synthesis of best practice principles. ★ denotes only in jurisdictions in which helmet use has been made mandatory.

Source: Fishman (2014).

have to use bike share? Is it faster than competing travel options? Is it more pleasant to use? Is it cheaper than other forms of transport? Are docking stations located close to where people live, work and shop? Does it feel safe to use? Is sign up easy and fast? Can users integrate bike share with public transport easily? Designing a system with these questions in mind is crucial to the success of a future bike share program, and these questions are discussed in more detail below.

12.1 Safety

As highlighted earlier, safety concerns are the primary reason people choose not to cycle, and people that do not currently cycle are even *more* sensitive to levels of protection from motorised transport than current cyclists. In terms of best practice, London, Paris and New York City (among others) all embarked on bicycle infrastructure campaigns in the years prior to the establishment of bike share. This infrastructure included a large number of separated bicycle facilities, and these helped to provide prospective users with the confidence necessary to start using the bike share system, helping to make streets safer for all road users and boosting the attractiveness of bike share.

In Paris, the infrastructure also included many targeted 'contra-flow' lanes that allowed two-way travel for cyclists, but only one-way travel for motorists. This helps to increase the value proposition for bike share over motorised forms of travel. In London, a large number of separated bicycle lanes that extend for many kilometres have now been added to the network, helping to provide safe conditions for cycling. By contrast, very little bicycle infrastructure was developed in the planning of the bike share programs in Melbourne and Brisbane, and both have a level of hostility to prospective cyclists, to the point that it has detracted from usability (Fishman, 2014). The overwhelming theme emerging from the international assessment of bike share program success is that a substantial investment in separated, connected bicycle lanes and paths need to be constructed, as well as a lowering of speed limits before bike share is likely to succeed. In a survey to members of the public in Brisbane, 'More bike lanes and paths' received the highest mean score when non–bike share members were asked 'What factors would encourage you to become a CityCycle member?' (Fishman, 2014). Moreover, in addition to helping to bolster the bike share program itself, these lanes and paths will also help to increase road safety, for all road users, including those cycling on private bikes.

Finally, it is possible for bike share planners to forget that not all adults know how to ride a bike, and an even greater proportion may not feel comfortable riding, as it may have been decades since their last ride. When preparing for the launch of a new bike share program, or when promoting an existing one, it may be necessary to hold 'come and try' days, in car-free locations, to enable people to experience bike share in a controlled environment, with staff on hand to assist inexperienced riders. Such events, in addition to improving safety, may also act as an awareness raising scheme, helping to bolster usage in the crucial early phase of a bike share program.

12.2 Convenience

The most consistent finding in the international literature on bike share is that people choose to use bike share when it meets their *convenience* criteria. In practice, this means that docking stations need to be close to their home, workplace and other destinations they frequently visit. It might also help explain why dockless bike share has been so popular in many cities. Seattle's dockless bike share providers have had many more trips taken in 6 months than the earlier docked system (*Pronto*), partly because people are able to drop bikes much closer to their final destination. Moreover, because dockless systems are cheaper to produce, a set budget will always buy more dockless than docked bikes, meaning the system will be larger.

Best practice bike share cities, in addition to providing relatively large systems, have also worked to integrate them into the existing public transport service. Data on user attitudes and behaviour show a very strong desire to make multimodal journeys that involve segments of walking, bike share and public transport. Although by no means an industry standard yet, integrating bike share access into public transport smartcard ticketing taps into a very strong user preference to have an access all modes pass that works on both bike share and other forms of public transport. The revamped Velib system in Paris is integrated with the *Navigo* smartcard public transport pass. Emerging technological developments allow bike share users to be able to access both bike share and public transport through the use of a single smartphone app. City planners must also be cognisant of the fact that not all citizens that may be interested in using bike share have access to a credit card or smartphone. Creating special programs to assist these individuals to join bike share will help broaden the demographic profile of users.

Ultimately, what much of the research and user surveys suggest is that bike share needs to be time competitive with competing modes. This is especially the case for commuting trips (in which users are more time sensitive). Convenience is all about the value proposition. What is the value proposition bike share offers a potential user? Central to the success of bike share therefore is the degree to which bike share competes with car use for short to medium car trips. If car use is faster, door to door, it will be difficult to attract people to bike share. Thinking about the bike share service in relation to competing modes is central to its ability to provide the level of convenience necessary to attract ridership.

12.3 Spontaneity

The average bike share trip is between 12 and 16 minutes in duration (Fishman, 2015). These short trips are very often not planned well in advance. Programs that require a user to sign up days in advance have lost large numbers of potential users. Generally, existing best practice is to allow for credit card swipe/tap sign up, that offers immediate access to the user, 24/7. Moreover, mandatory helmet legislation can hamper the spontaneity with which people seek bike share.

In Brisbane, especially in the early phase, users were asked to listen to over 20 minutes of legal disclaimer notices and were not permitted to use the system after 10 pm or before 5 am. These factors severely limited the ability of new users to sign up as fast as they would have liked, with many forgoing the opportunity. Moreover, mandatory helmet use hampered the spontaneity with which people could use the bike share systems in Australia and the handful of other jurisdictions in which a blanket helmet law applies. No city with a well-enforced mandatory helmet law has run a bike share system averaging more than one trip per day, per bike.

Finally, as identified in this book on several occasions, the strongest marketing tool for a new bike share program is *seeing someone else using the system*. For this reason, it is vital that everything be done from launch to incentivise early use. Having bike share bikes sitting idle must be minimised. This can be achieved by having a 'brand champion' (such as a local sporting hero or other celebrity), come and try days, ambassadors and pricing to incentivise early use (e.g., half-price memberships for people who sign up with a friend). Seeing others using the system will create the social norm that will allow other people to see the possibility of using the system and sign up spontaneously.

References

Fishman, E. (2014). *Bikeshare: Barriers, facilitators and impacts on car use* (PhD thesis by publication). Queensland University of Technology, Brisbane.

Fishman, E. (2015). Bikeshare: A review of recent literature. *Transport Reviews*, 1–22. doi:10.1080/01441647.2015.1033036

13 Conclusion

The proportion of the global population living in cities has never been higher, and this trend is set to magnify by 2050, when over 70% of the world's population will be urban. It is clear that if we wish to continue this transition to urban settlement in a manner that advances economic productivity and prosperity, in addition to the more important objectives of human health and environmental well-being, we need to make some substantial reforms to city planning. Traffic congestion and time spent commuting is one of the most frustrating aspects of modern city life, resulting in lost productivity and reducing the quality of life for millions. The private car is the most space inefficient mode of transport (United Nations, 2013), and mass car use clearly does not scale up well to provide efficient movement in big cities (Walker, 2016).

The car promised to rid cities of the problems caused by horses. Yet as population health experts have been identifying for several decades, the car has its own set of no less significant problems for human health. Three times as many people die each year due to road traffic crashes than malaria (World Health Organisation, 2015, 2016). Air pollution caused by motorised transport is a significant and growing problem; estimated to cause up to 70% of total urban air pollution (World Health Organisation, 2017), killing millions annually.

Climate change threatens the viability of human habitation. The French President recently declared that the world is losing the war against climate change (Macron, 2017) and according to the International Panel on Climate Change, the way we transport ourselves has become one of the major, and fastest growing, sources of greenhouse gas emissions (Sims et al., 2014). Car use is the major component within general transport emissions and, compared to other modes of transport (e.g. aviation) has the most capacity for mode shift, to lower emissions intensive forms of transport.

Given the seriousness and magnitude of the issues outlined above, there has never been a better time to challenge the dominance of the automobile era. The automobile age, which has dominated city planning for over 60 years, has in fact never been under greater threat. The era in which automobile companies were able to sell a car to every adult with a decent income (and plenty to those without one) may be drawing to a close.

The proportion of young adults owning a car is declining in many OECD countries (Delbosc & Currie, 2013), and technology has now advanced to the point in which it may become more attractive to simply 'summon' a vehicle when needed, helping to lower car ownership (and hopefully), usage. Former Ford CEO Mark Fields when talking about the future of mobility whilst still CEO said: 'We look at changing consumer buying behaviours, particularly millennials in urban areas. They want access versus ownership' (Ziegler & Patel, 2016).

Bike share has emerged over the last decade as one of the most exciting prospects for offering low carbon, healthy, affordable mobility to the growing global population of city dwellers (Fishman, 2014). In big, congested cities, bike share can offer a time-competitive alternative to car use, and greater freedom than often crowded public transport. Shanghai provides an example of what bike share can achieve. Within the space of 2 years, after the introduction of more than a million bike share bikes, the proportion of trips by pedal power jumped from 5% to 12%.

Combining public transport and bike share can offer the best of both worlds, and it is clear that many bike share users are choosing to integrate with public transport, helping to make up for the inherent weaknesses in each. Convenience is the most consistently repeated reason why people use bike share. Designing a user-orientated system that taps into people's need for being able to ride spontaneously, safely and with door-to-door convenience is central to the overall success of bike share. It is also clear that people do not make decisions to use bike share in isolation from other modes. If a city plans its transport system with the intention of making car use convenient and affordable, it will always be very difficult for bike share to succeed as anything other than a fun thing for tourists.

Whilst safety concerns continue to be a major barrier to greater numbers of people using bike share, the evidence thus far is that bike share is safer than private bike use (Fishman & Schepers, 2016). Improvements in bicycle infrastructure are a challenge all but a handful of Dutch and Danish cities need to address urgently. The gains in cities like New York and London have been impressive over recent years, and bike share appears to act as a catalyst for cities to begin a step change in their level of investment in bike lanes and paths. In this regard, bike share may be having a transformative effect on cities. Prior to the launch of Velib, few thought of Paris and a 'bike city' and yet now, Paris is re-inventing itself, in part through transport initiatives that re-prioritise street space for people over cars. For many Parisians, it would be difficult to think of life in the French capital now without 20,000 'little buses' that are used, up to six times a day, each.

By far the most radical change in bike share over the last 2 years has been the transformation from docked to dockless bike share. Large Chinese firms are leading this disruption, with fleets of millions of bicycles, all connected to the cloud in one form or another, with the ubiquity of the smartphone as the principal customer interface. It is difficult to overstate the magnitude of this shift towards dockless bike share. Prior to their emergence, it was not uncommon for cities to pay providers/operators $4,000–$8,000 per bike plus an extra $2,000 per year in operating costs for docked bike share. Now, cities are beginning to charge operators for the right to run a bike share service in their city.

It is not clear how economically sustainable this new form of bike share is and what the market might look like 2 years from now, as of early 2019, it does appear dockless bike share will continue to dominate the sector for the foreseeable future. Dockless bike share has come as a challenge to city planners, and more will need to be done to prepare cities to be able to absorb the bicycles that can often be produced for as little as $60 a unit. Determining the most appropriate number of bikes a city should have, and where they should park is a responsibility city governments must now tackle. They need to make the rules!

Ultimately, the ability of bike share to deliver benefits will be related to the degree to which it acts as a replacement for car use. Cities need to view bike share in terms of what it offers in meeting their wider strategic objectives. What does X city [insert your city] want to be like in 50 years from now? When most people are asked this question, they come up with a similar picture in their mind. A sustainable city, a city that has clean air and healthy citizens. A city that is accessible without the need to get in a car, for every trip. Bike share has a big role to play in the city of the future. City politicians and planners need to think strategically about what they can do now, to help transform their city into the one they would like to leave for their children and grandchildren, 50 years from now. There has never been more opportunity or more reason to start planning better cities, and bike share is a great tool to help achieve the city we all want for the future.

References

Delbosc, A., & Currie, G. (2013). Causes of youth licensing decline: A synthesis of evidence. Transport Reviews, 33(3), 271–290. doi:10.1080/01441647.2013.801929

Fishman, E. (2014). Bikeshare: Barriers, facilitators and impacts on car use (PhD thesis by publication). Queensland University of Technology, Brisbane.

Fishman, E., & Schepers, P. (2016). Global bike share: What the data tells us about road safety. Journal of Safety Research, 56, 41–45.

Macron, E. (2017). Emmanuel Macron Says the World is Losing the Battle against Climate Change. Retrieved from http://www.abc.net.au/news/2017-12-13/we-are-losing-the-battle-french-president-tells-climate-summit/9254862

Sims, R., Schaeffer, R., Creutzig, F., Cruz-Núñez, X., D'Agosto, M., Dimitriu, D., … Tiwari, G. (2014). Transport. In Climate Change 2014: Mitigation of Climate Change. Contribution of Working Group III to the Fifth Assessment Report of the Intergovernmental Panel on Climate Change. Retrieved from https://www.ipcc.ch/site/assets/uploads/2018/02/ipcc_wg3_ar5_chapter8.pdf

United Nations. (2013). Review of Developments in Transport in Asia and the Pacific. Retrieved from http://www.unescap.org/sites/default/files/TransportReview_2013_full_text.pdf

Walker, J. (Producer). (2016). Why cars and cities are a bad match [Opinion piece]. Retrieved from https://www.washingtonpost.com/news/in-theory/wp/2016/03/02/buses-and-trains-thats-what-will-solve-congestion/

World Health Organisation. (2015). Global Status Report on Road Safety 2015. Retrieved from http://www.who.int/violence_injury_prevention/road_safety_status/2015/en/

World Health Organisation. (2016). 10 Facts on Malaria. Retrieved from http://www.who.int/features/factfiles/malaria/en/

World Health Organisation. (2017). Air Pollution. Retrieved from http://www.who.int/sustainable-development/transport/health-risks/air-pollution/en/

Ziegler, C., & Patel, N. (2016). Meet the New Ford, a Silicon Valley Software Company. Retrieved from https://www.theverge.com/2016/4/7/11333288/ford-ceo-mark-fields-interview-electric-self-driving-car-software

Index

Note: **Bold** page numbers refer to tables; *italic* page numbers refer to figures and page numbers followed by "n" denote endnotes.